A LITTLE BIRD TOLD ME

HarperNorth
Windmill Green
24 Mount Street
Manchester M2 3NX

A division of
HarperCollins*Publishers*
1 London Bridge Street
London SE1 9GF

www.harpercollins.co.uk

HarperCollins*Publishers*
Macken House, 39/40 Mayor Street Upper
Dublin 1, D01 C9W8, Ireland

Published by HarperCollins*Publishers* Ltd 2026

1 3 5 7 9 10 8 6 4 2

A catalogue record of this book is available from the British Library

HB ISBN 978-0-00-878159-0

Printed and bound in the UK using 100% renewable electricity
at CPI Group (UK) Ltd

A LITTLE BIRD TOLD ME

An illustrated compendium of bird phrases

MATT SEWELL

Harper North

For my goldfinches
Jess, Romy & Mae

For a Spotify playlist inspired
by the book, scan the code.

Contents

Introduction

Our coexistence with the avian world is central to who we are. Birds and their songs surround us all day and have become a part of our folklore and customs (Christmas Day, for many of us, would unfortunately feel empty without a stuffed bird – or partridges in pear trees). Bird-spotting is a national pastime and the mere sight of one can bring joy to the rest your day. And, of course, birds have become an integral part of our language, represented in expressions passed down across generations to help convey exactly what it is to be a human. Some of these phrases go back to biblical times and some are so everyday their true bird-related essence has been lost. So, it's fun to inspect the history and relevance of these idioms and to explore our love of birds a little bit more, just for a lark.

Is it all true? That's for the birds.

A bird in the hand

...is worth two in the bush. The second part of this phrase is a mystery to some. It's all about taking the easy road: 'just go for the bird in hand'. Be wise, like a poacher, rather than trying to be clever, making a noisy mess of it and losing everything.

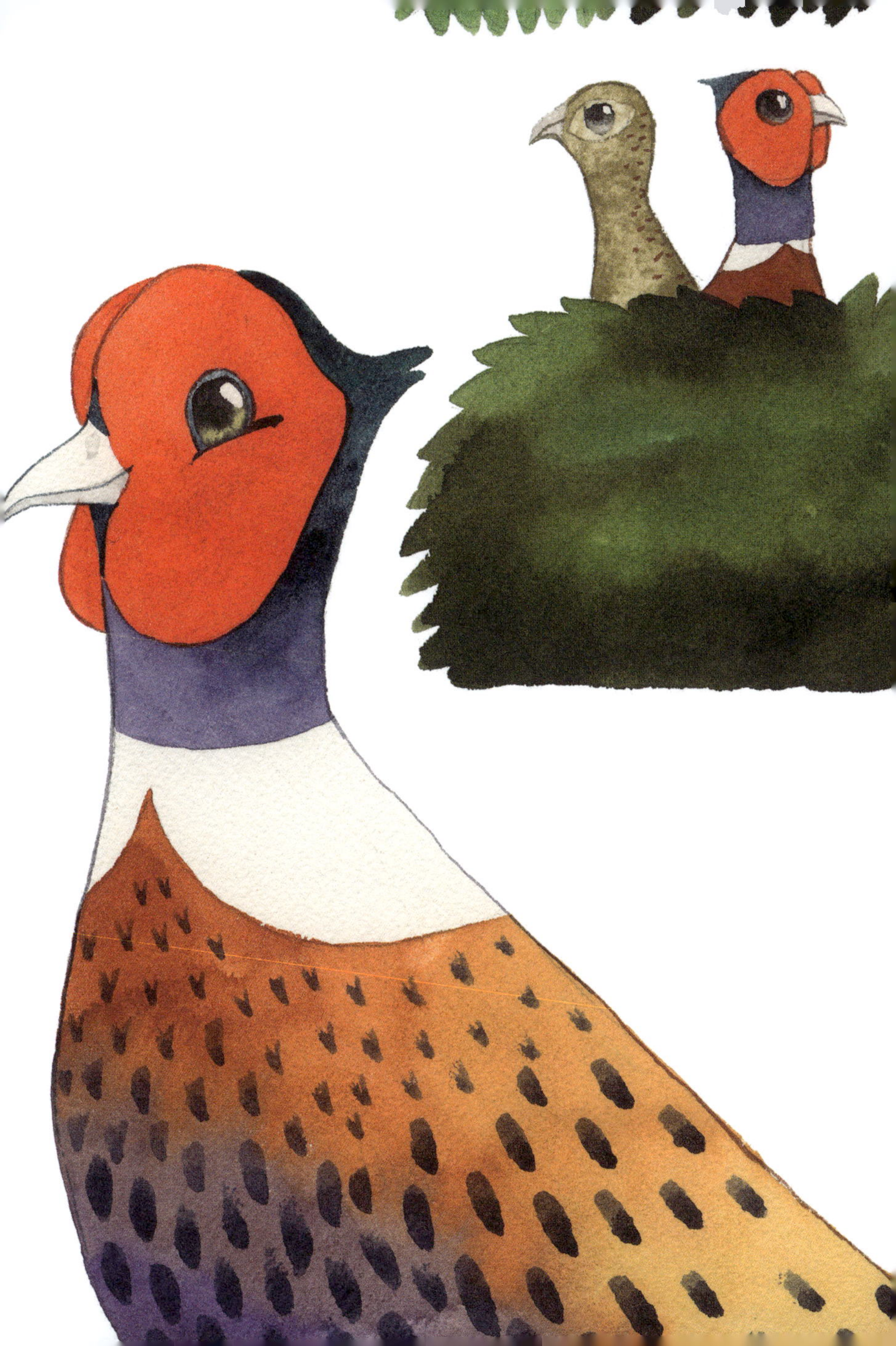

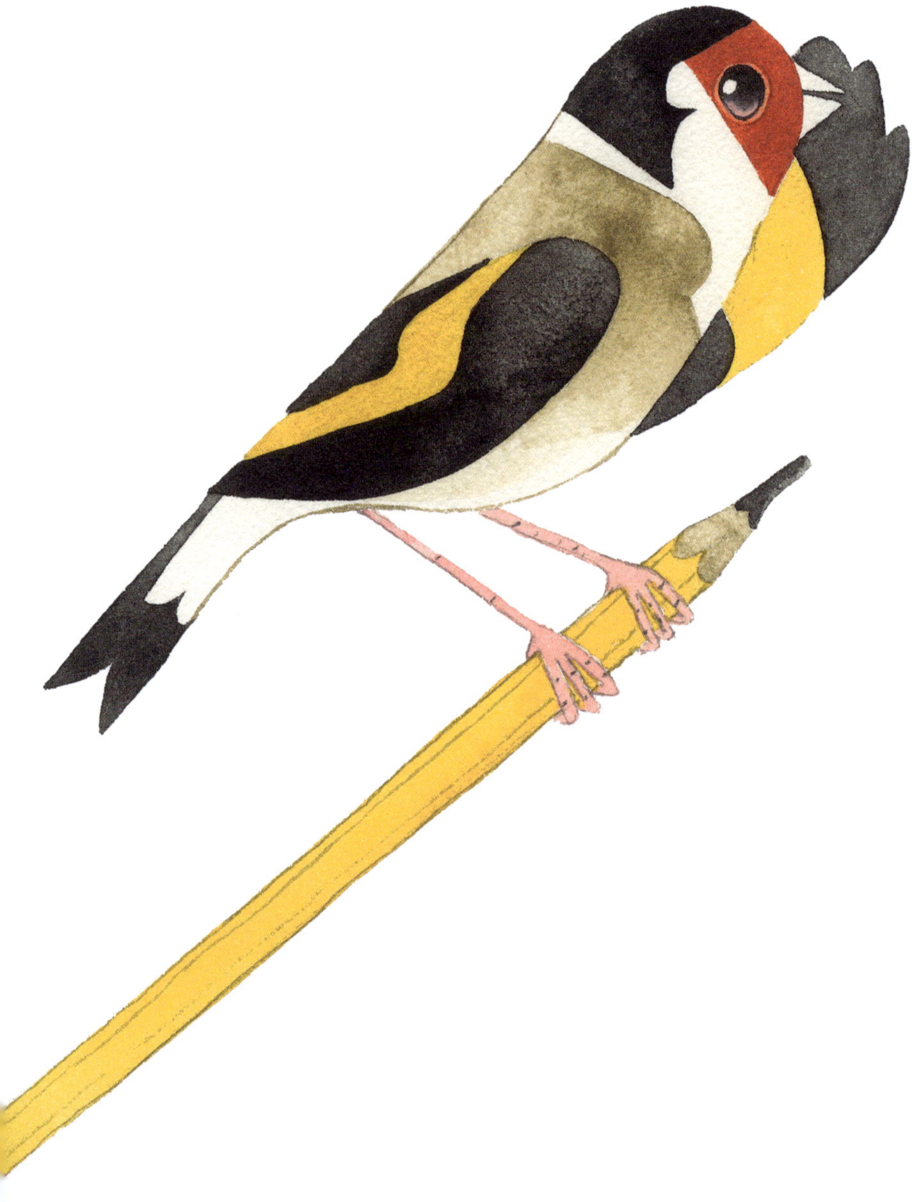

A little bird told me

—

If you love a good gossip, there is no better way to hide the source of your salacious rumours than by announcing you only know it because 'a little bird told you'. People have been hiding behind this handy little quip since biblical times, as it was written in the Old Testament that birds could repeat ill-spoken words in their cheery little songs. So don't gossip!

—

An albatross around one's neck

An ongoing burden in one's life. The phrase originates from an eighteenth-century epic by Samuel Taylor Coleridge. I can say I've known about the plight of this burdensome seabird since I was a youngster not because I read classical poetry, but because I was a teenage dirtbag who listened to Iron Maiden. In particular, the track 'Rime of the Ancient Mariner', a song based on the poem from which this saying was born.

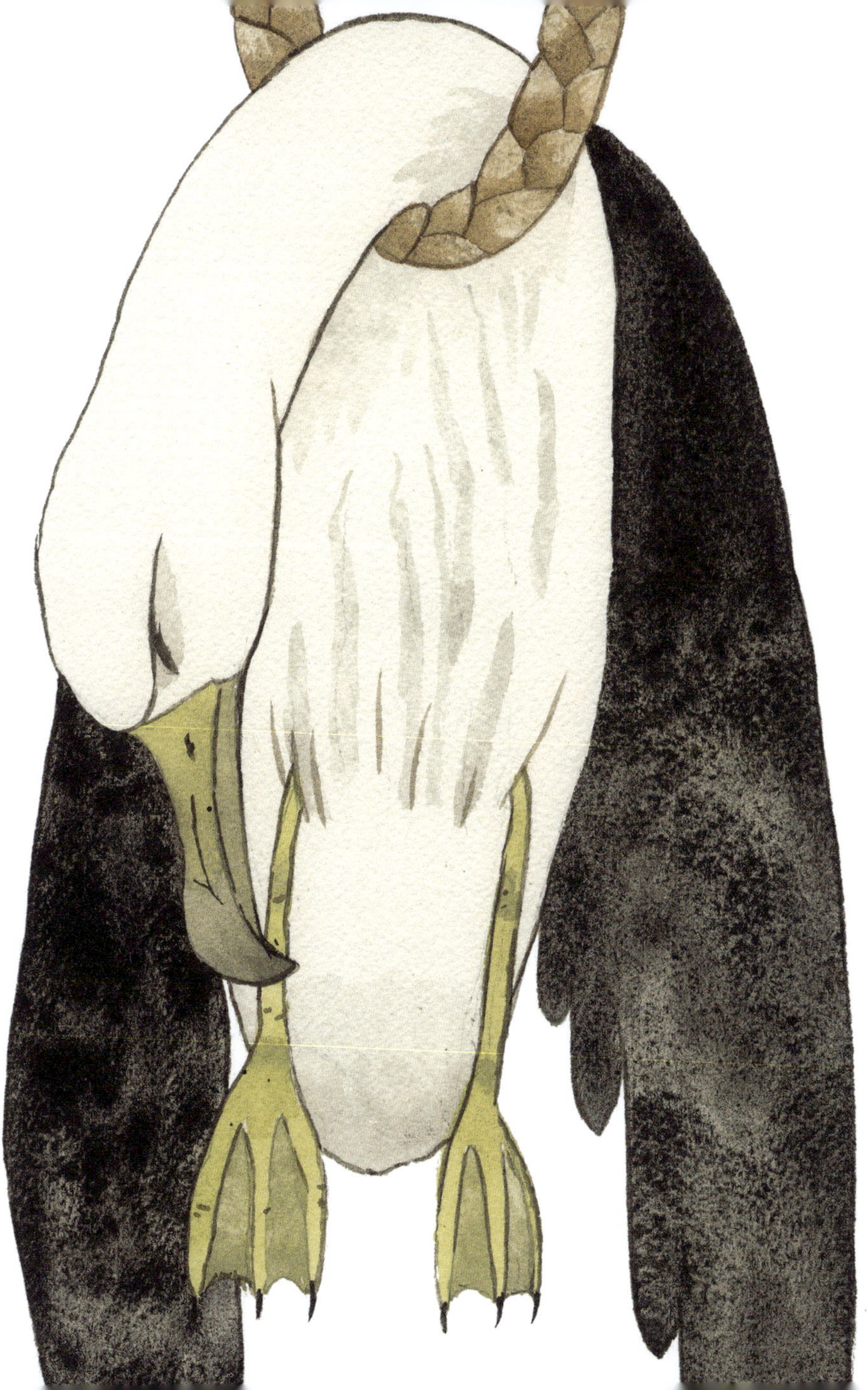

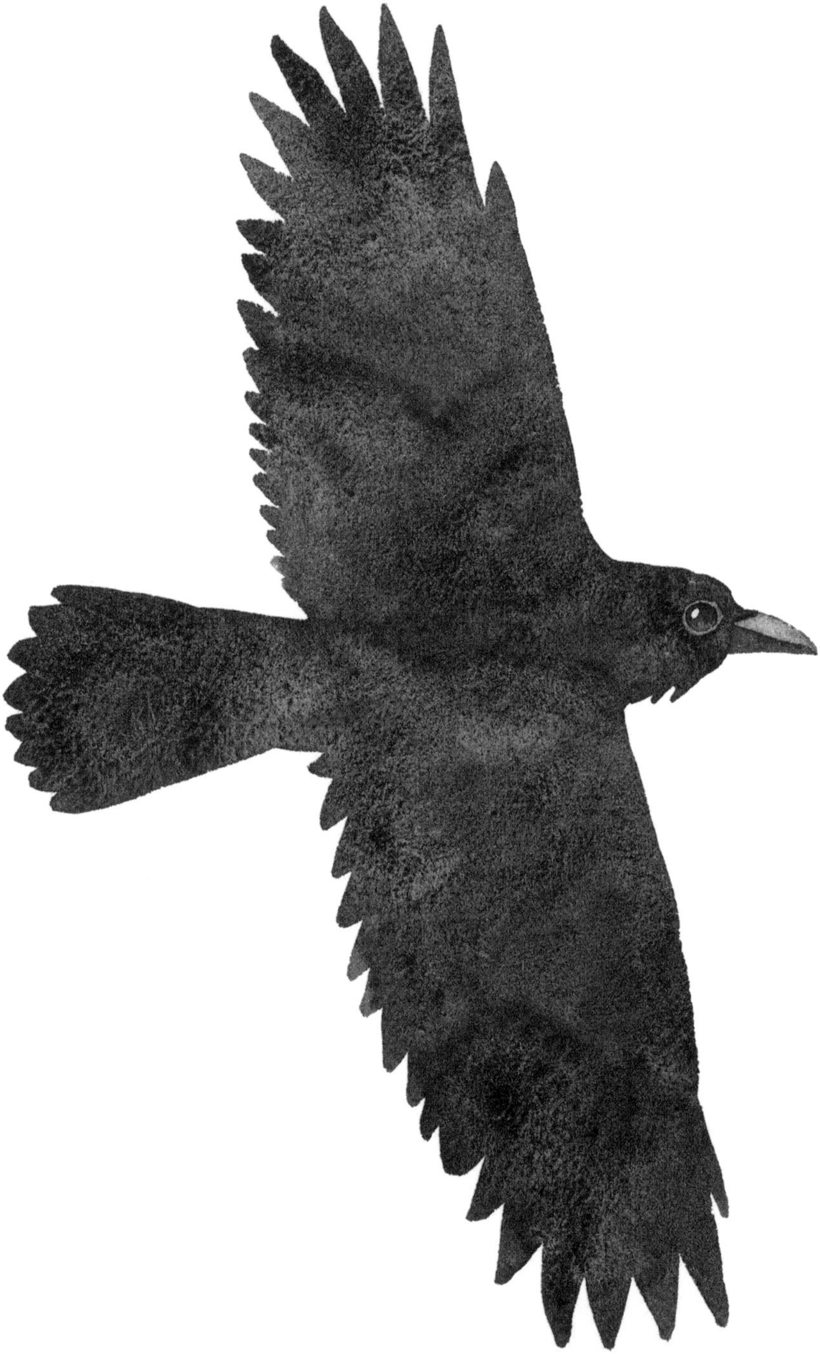

As the crow flies

Some birds fly in endless arcs, and some birds bounce (I'm looking at you, green woodpecker!). There are also birds that fly straight as an arrow, and the crow most definitely fits into this category. Meaning a straight line between two points, this folk saying has been around for hundreds of years.

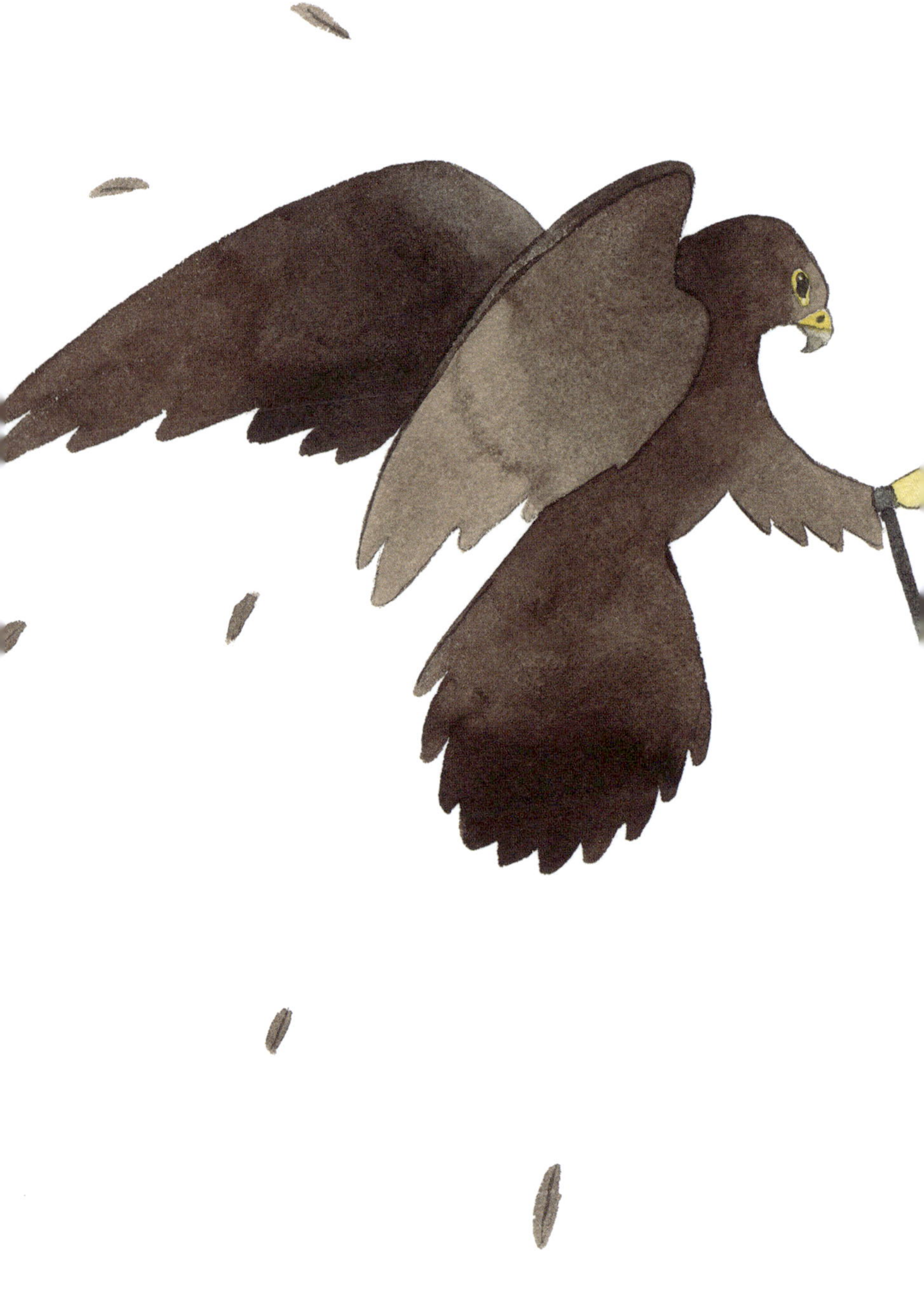

At the end of your tether

You've had just about as much as you can take and your patience has stretched to snapping point. Just like the hawk who is flapping desperately for freedom but is tethered to a post. This is another phrase originating from falconry, like waiting with 'bated breath', which was when an eager or hungry bird would be flapping boisterously and straining at the tether to get hunting.

Bald as a coot

The 'chrome-dome' referred to by this centuries-old idiom is a common waterside bird, the coot, found up and down the United Kingdom in parks, canals, rivers and lakes. Like the bird's other global family members, moorhens and swamp hens, coots aren't actually bald. They sport a glorious shiny frontal shield that is connected to the upper mandible of the beak – so not a slaphead in sight!

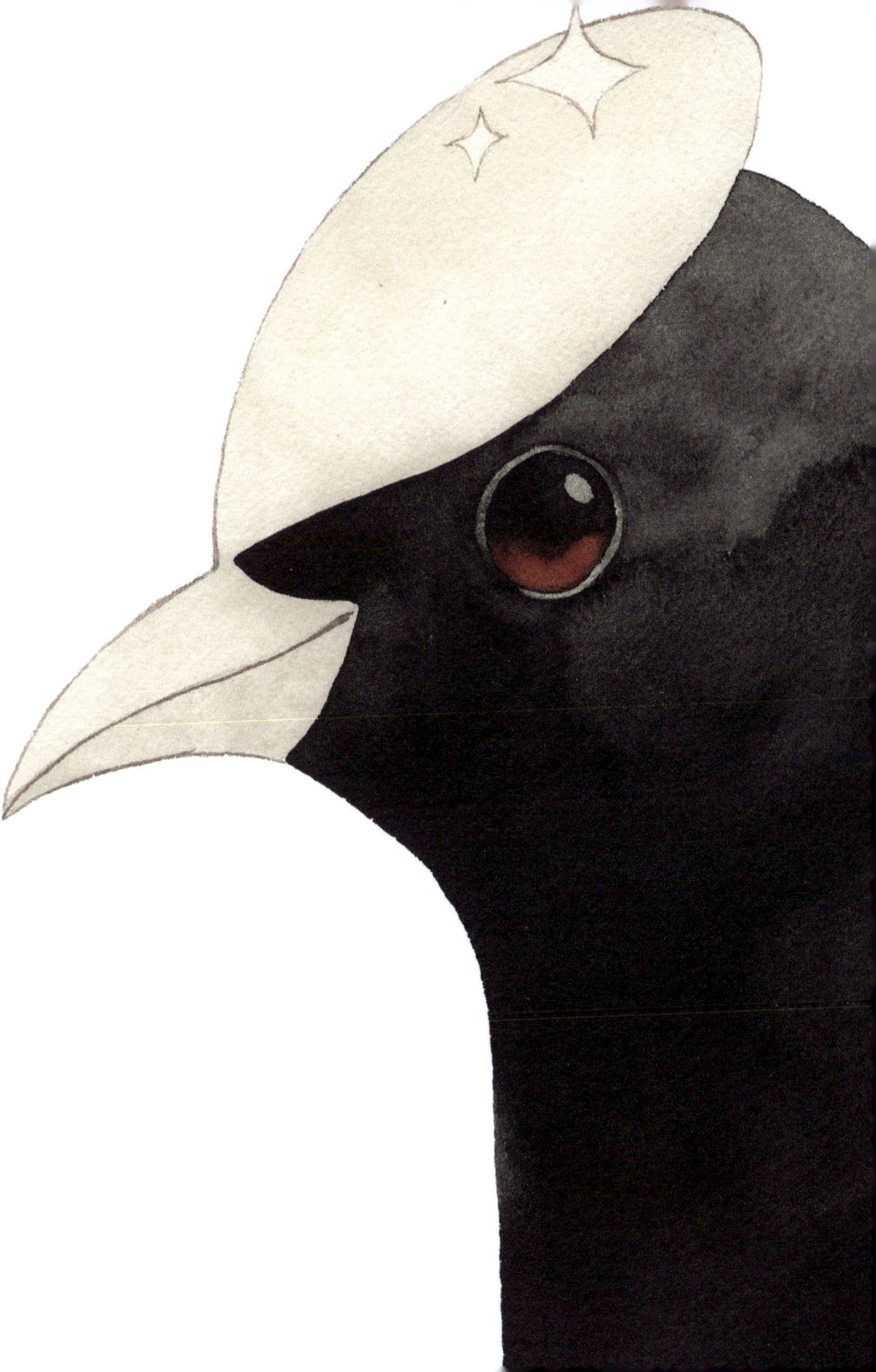

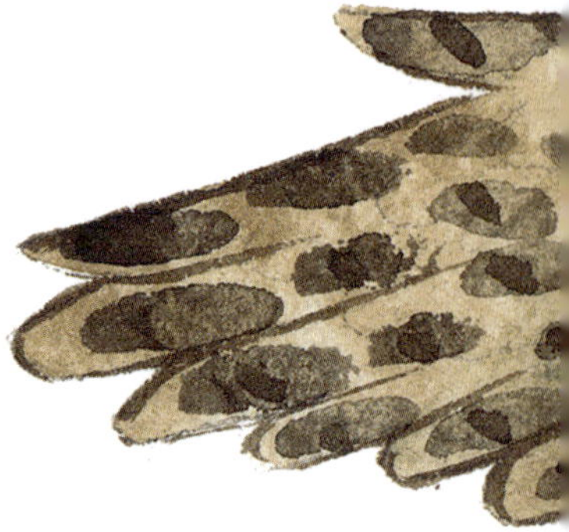

Bird’s-eye view

A bird’s-eye view is an overall picture.
A perspective of something directly overhead,
like a Christmas-gift drone before it is blown
catastrophically into the high branches of a tree,
or a hovering kestrel before it drops in a flash
upon an unsuspecting shrew.

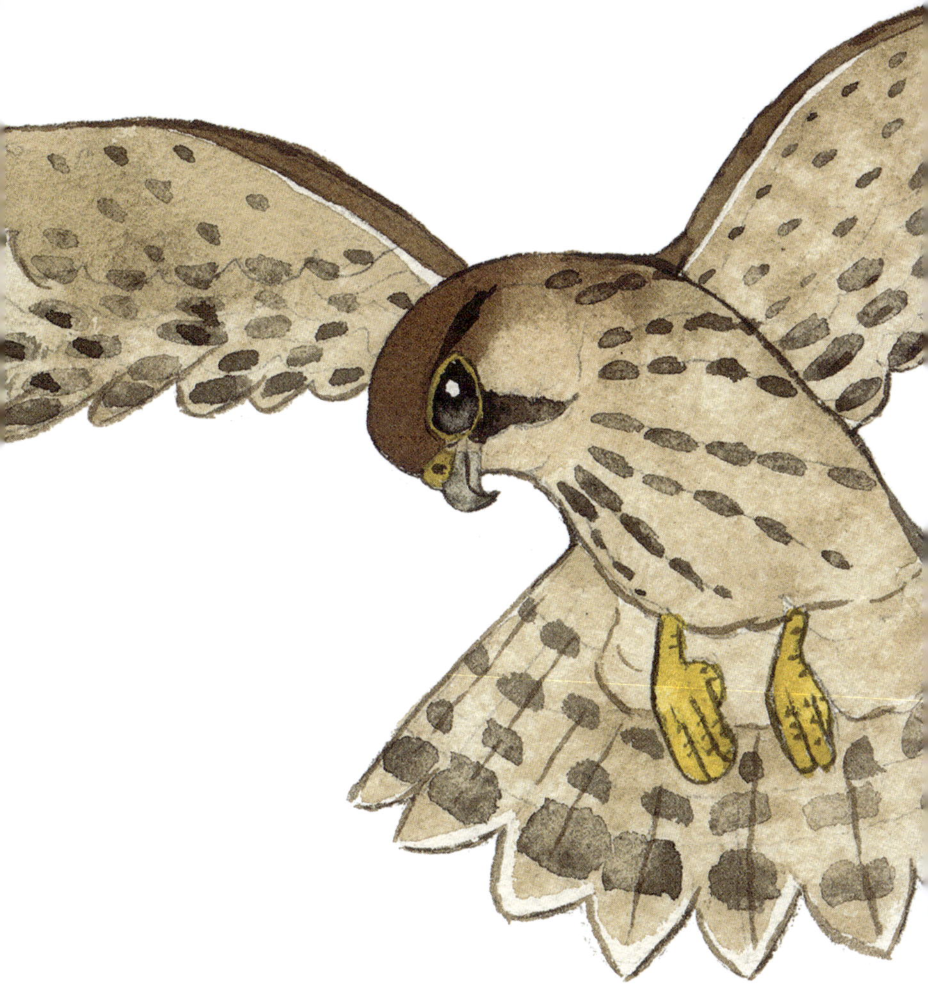

Birds of a feather flock together

People are like birds in so many ways; we can be flighty and migratory, keen to build nests or all too happy to belt out a song. And just as birds of the same species can gather in flocks, we are also drawn to crowds of similar fashions, tastes, beliefs and outlooks. It seems like we've always been this way, as the saying goes back to biblical times and beyond.

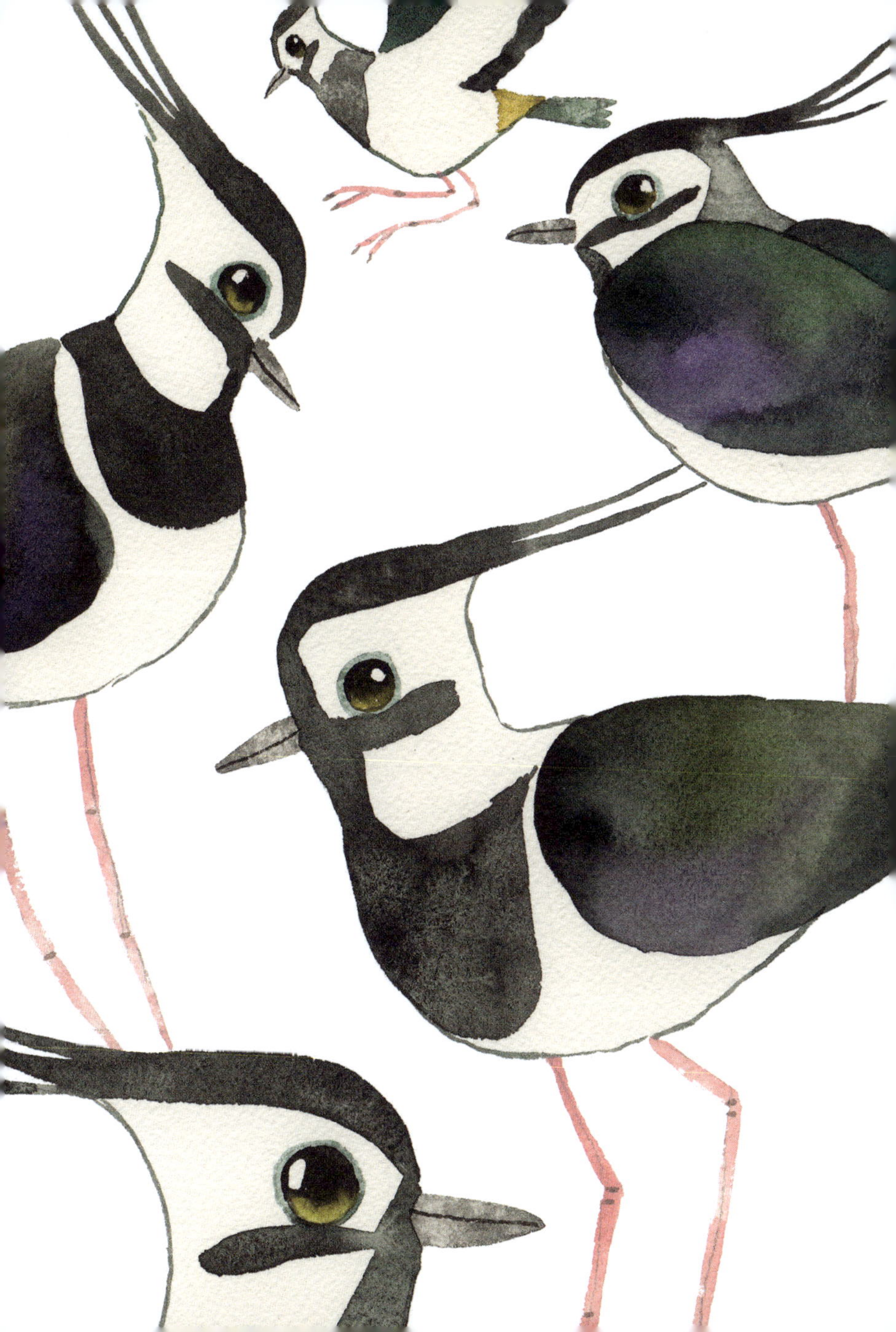

Black swan event

Not many things in life are certain, but some things you can comfortably lay your trust upon: the sun rising each morning; rain in the school summer holidays; the fact that swans are white. But this illusion was shattered when European colonisers returned from Australasia in the late 1600s with tales of black swans. Minds were duly blown by this revelation, so earth-shatteringly bonkers that subsequent unimaginably unique and unthinkable things have gone on to be described as a 'black swan event'.

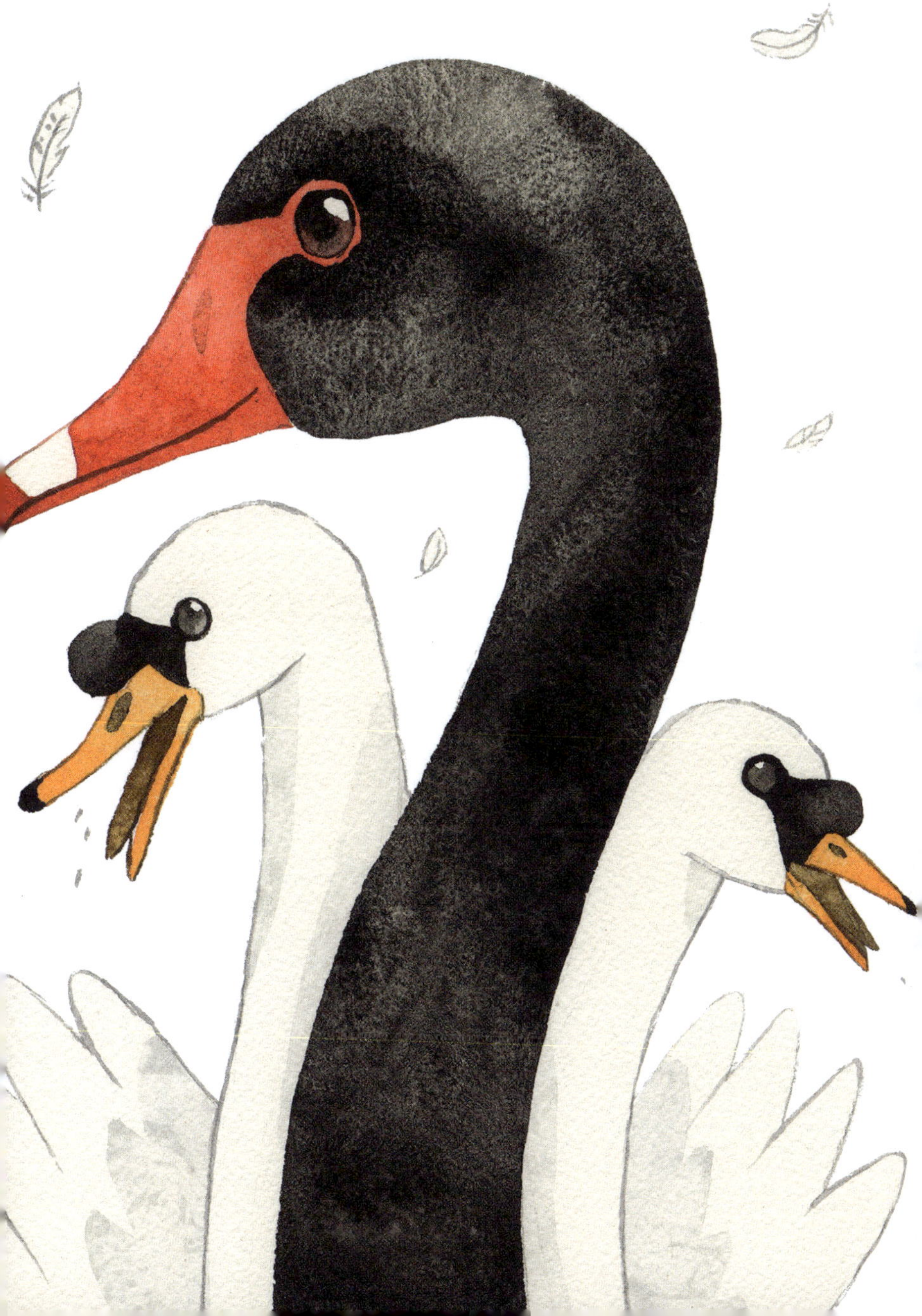

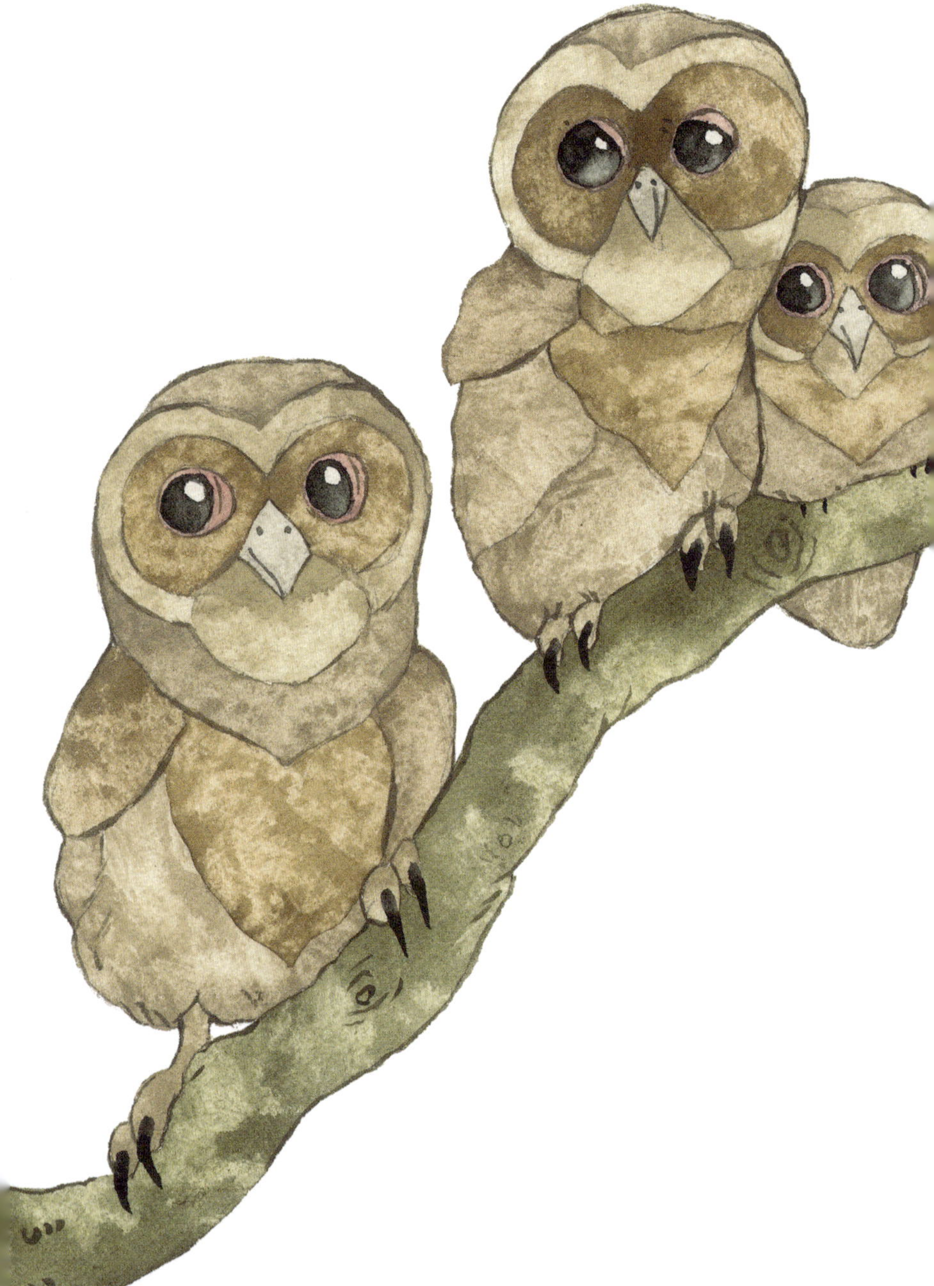

Branching out

Sporting badly-applied mascara and itching to meet up with friends, pre-nagers have a leash slowly let out longer over a period of time, testing their reliability before they hit the town unescorted. Fledgling birds take similarly cautious ventures from the nest out onto the limbs of trees. This is particularly true of owlets, who push themselves further and further, branching out until they take that maiden flight.

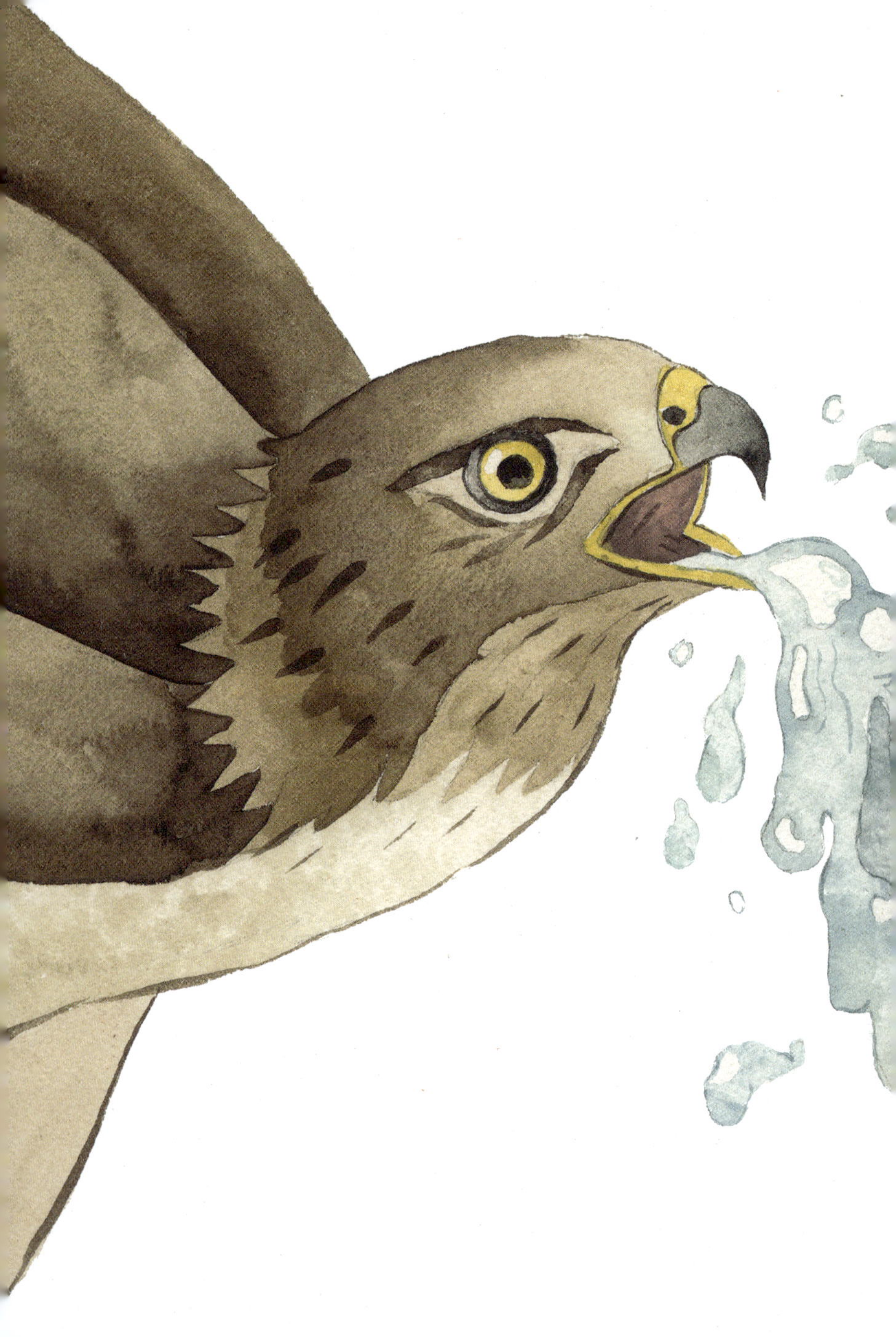

Boozer

Another of the many astonishing phrases originating from falconry parlance. In medieval times, a hawk or falcon that drank a lot of water was known to 'bowse'. Now, thanks to the passage of time, a heavy drinker is often now referred to as a boozer. Cheers!

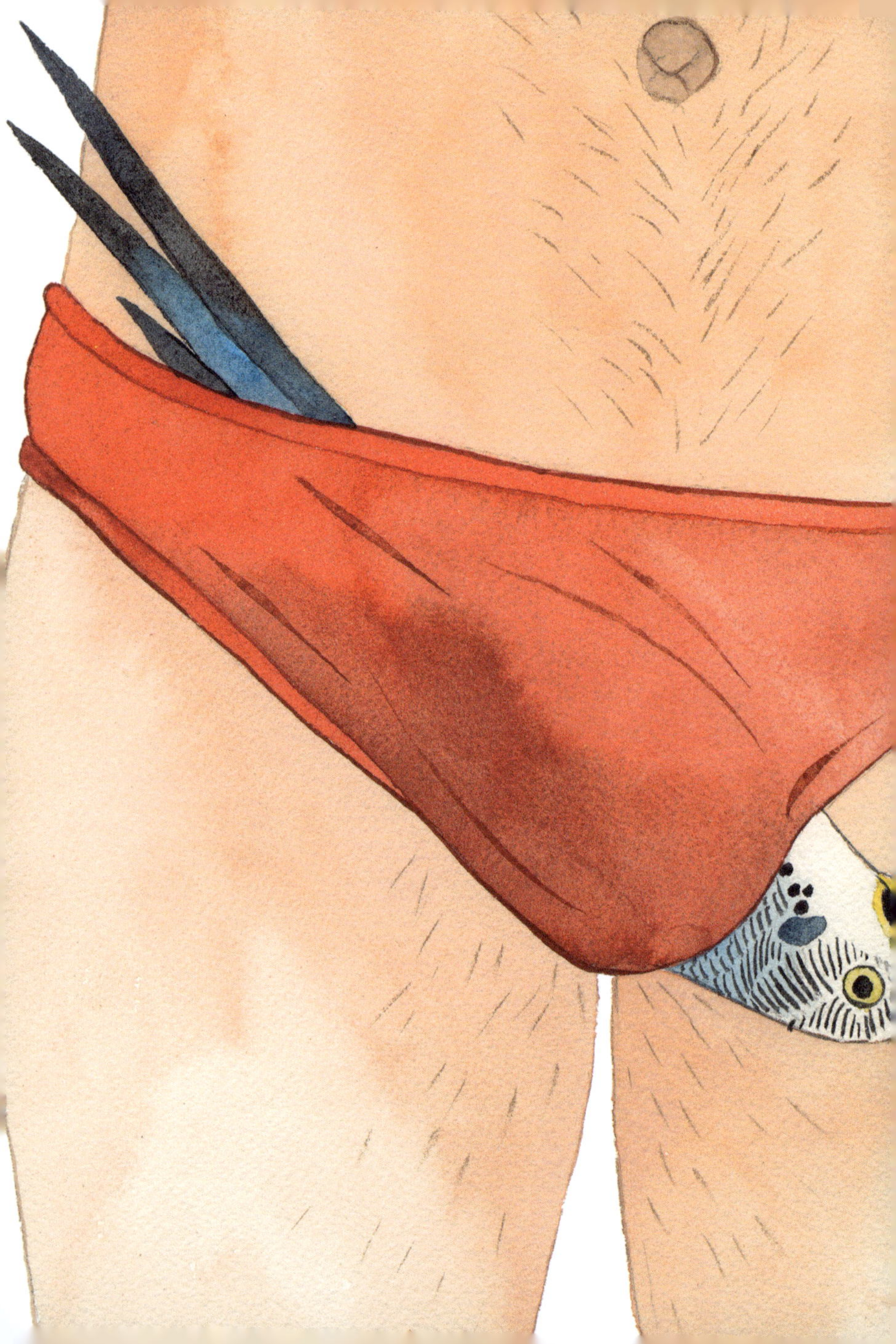

Budgie smuggler

Aussies have lots of amazing sayings, and the best feature birds, 'filthy drongo' or a 'flamin' galah' amongst them. This great expression describes those oh-so-tight swimming trunks made popular in the 80s and 90s and originates from down under. Now it has spread around the world, much like the native budgie that has become a worldwide pet.

Chickenshit

A startled hen is a sound familiar to anyone living close to a chicken coop, and oh my are they easily alarmed. The cowardice of a chicken has been enshrined in our language since the since the fourteenth century. Being 'chicken-hearted', 'chickening out' and 'playing chicken' are all fine ways to call out a coward, but the more recent 'chickenshit' is surely the champion of phrases.

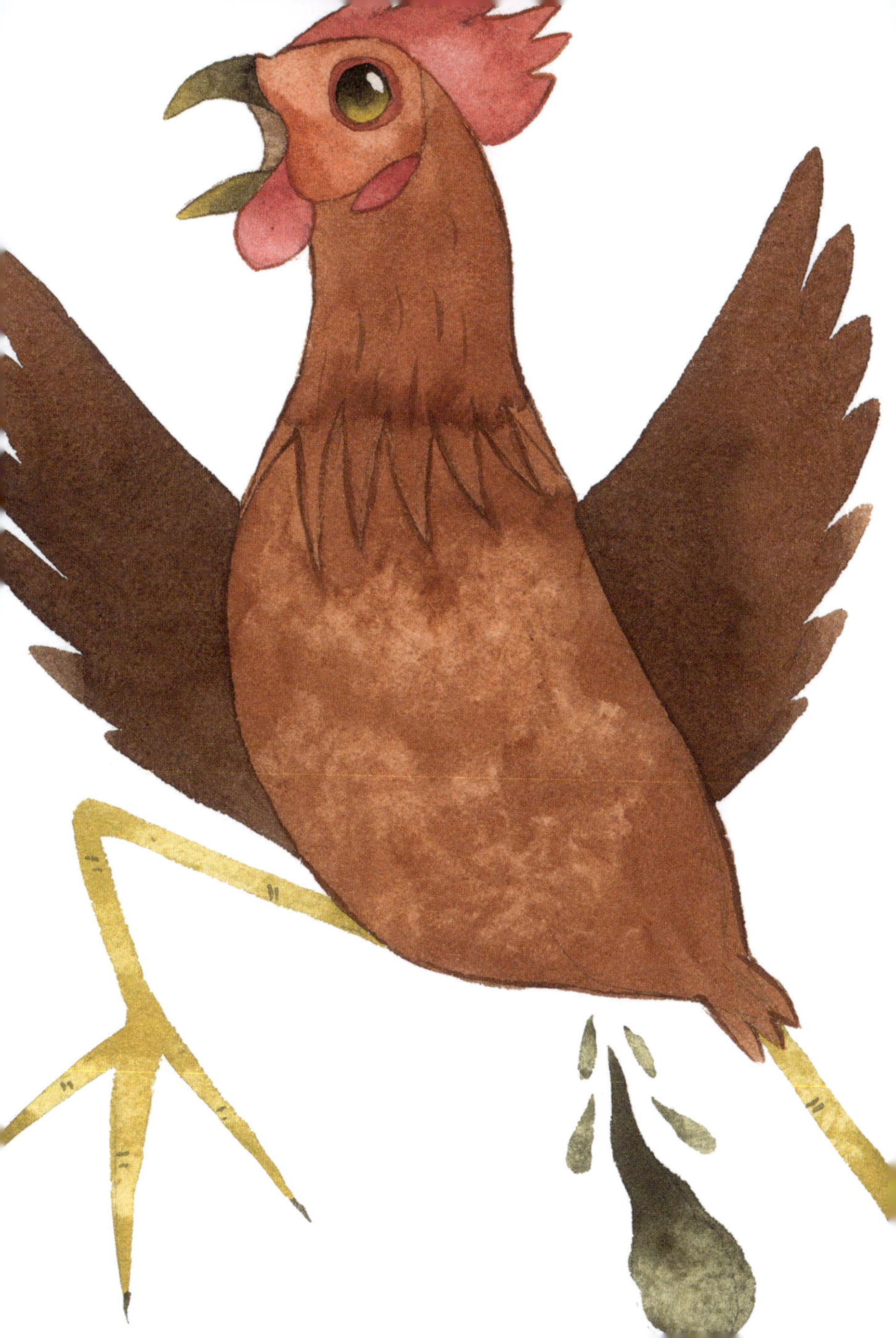

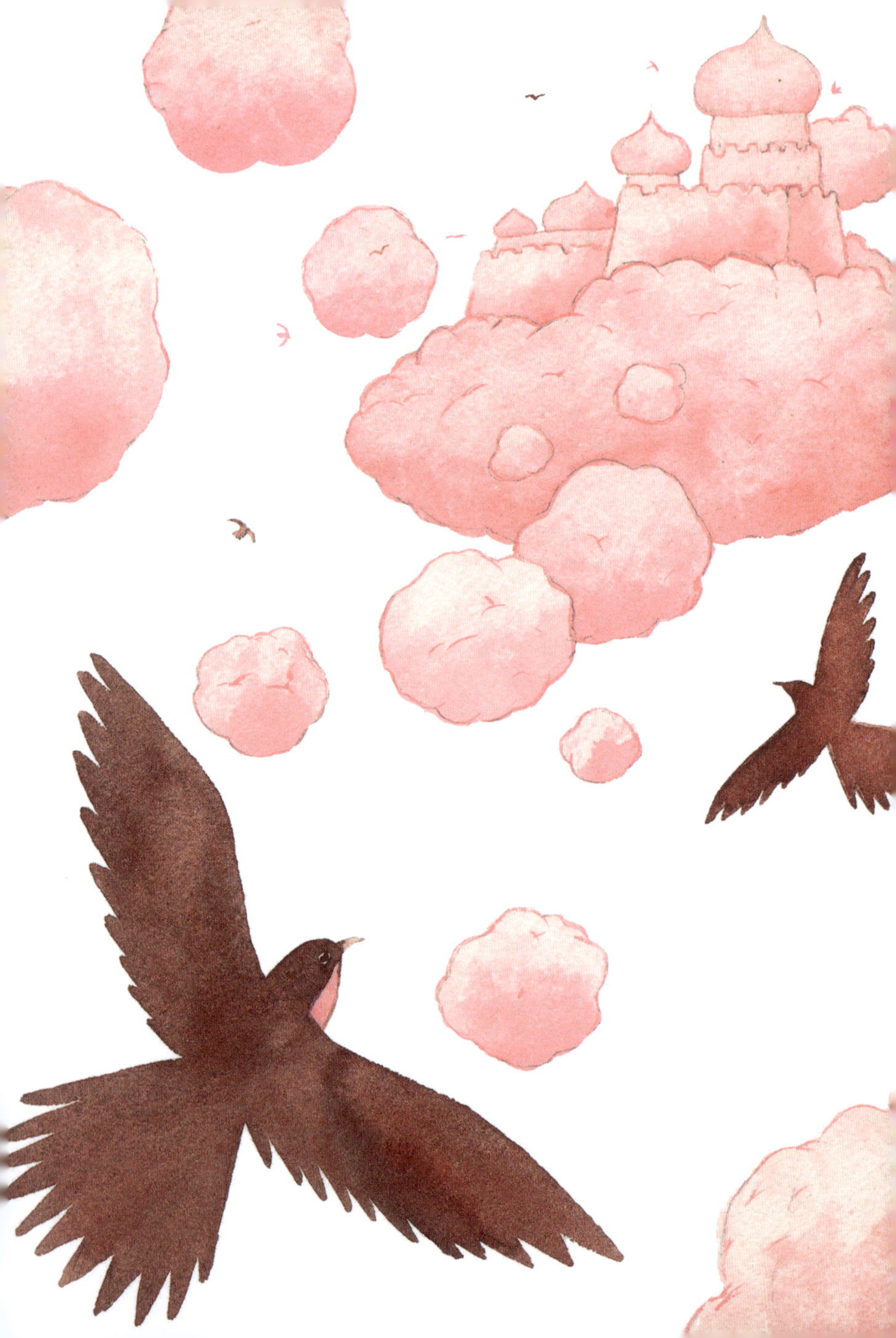

Cloud cuckoo land

Referring to someone as being 'a bit cuckoo' for acting weird, or maybe even slightly deranged, has been in popular parlance for hundreds of years. But if someone is partial to fantastical thoughts or living in denial, they are said to live in 'cloud cuckoo land' – a saying that originated in Ancient Greece from a play about a utopian bird-built city in the sky.

Cuckold

A cuckold is the powerless husband of a cheating wife. Emasculating and shameful, this is a term that goes back to medieval times and alludes to the parasitical nature of the female cuckoo, who will lay eggs in other birds' nests. In recent years the meaning of the phrase has morphed, instead describing a man who is bootlicking and submissive. Expressing opposing negative beliefs can also get you labeled a 'cuck'.

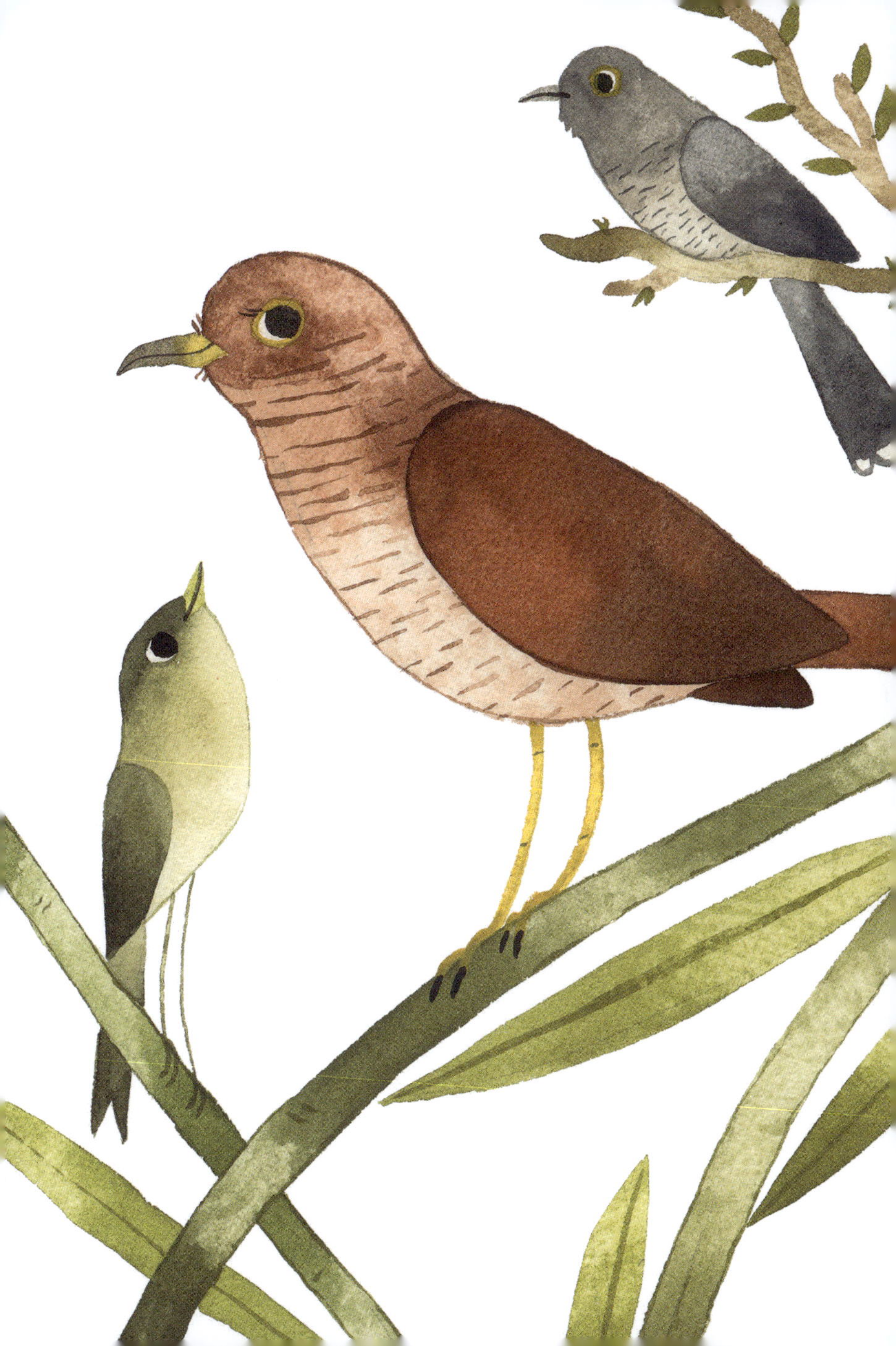

Culture vulture

Someone who loves to soak up the arts, devouring paintings, opera, plays, concerts and film with a ferocious appetite. 'Culture' handily rhymes with 'vulture', but the two words are also a perfect match, as the bird is known to voraciously pick at prey in a frenzied manner – much like a culture vulture, who may not actually be as discerning an art lover as they first appear.

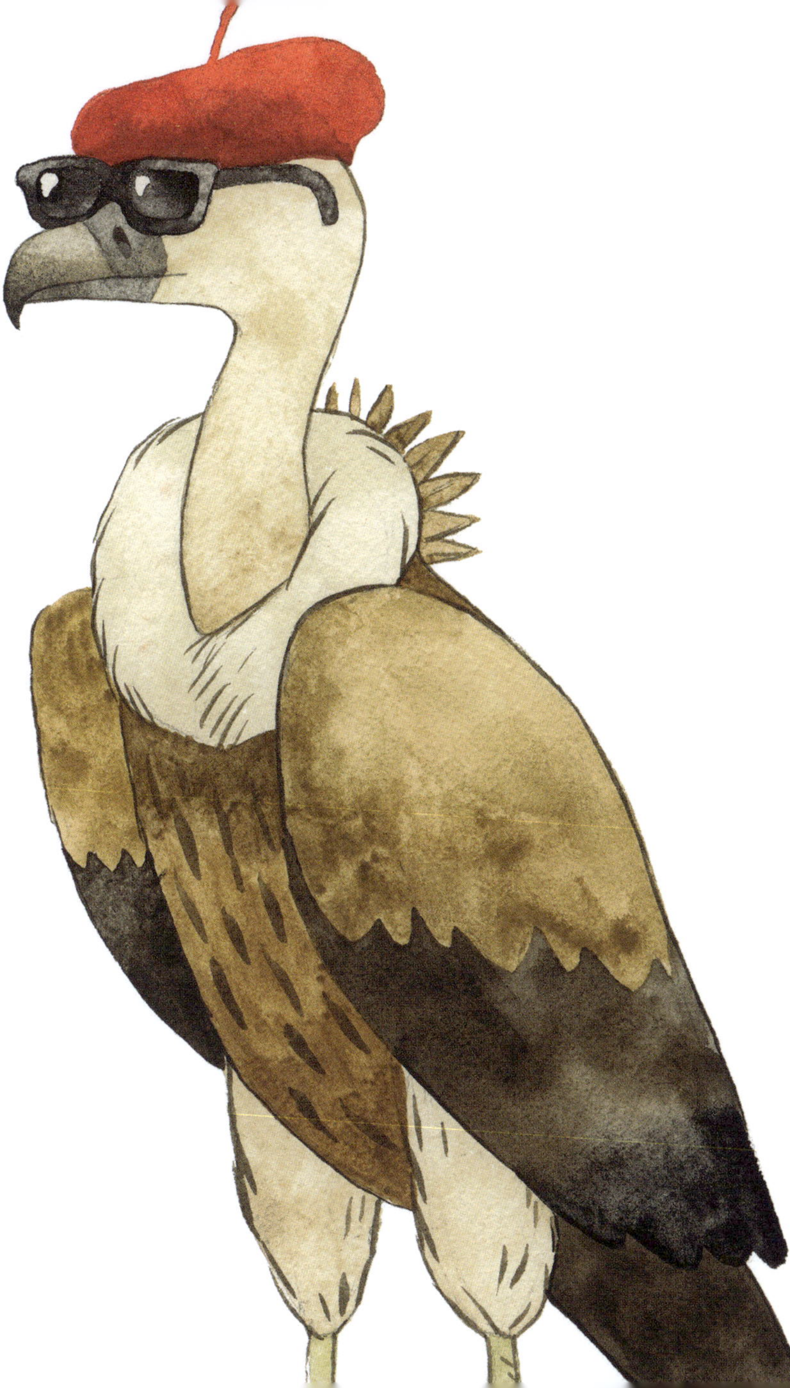

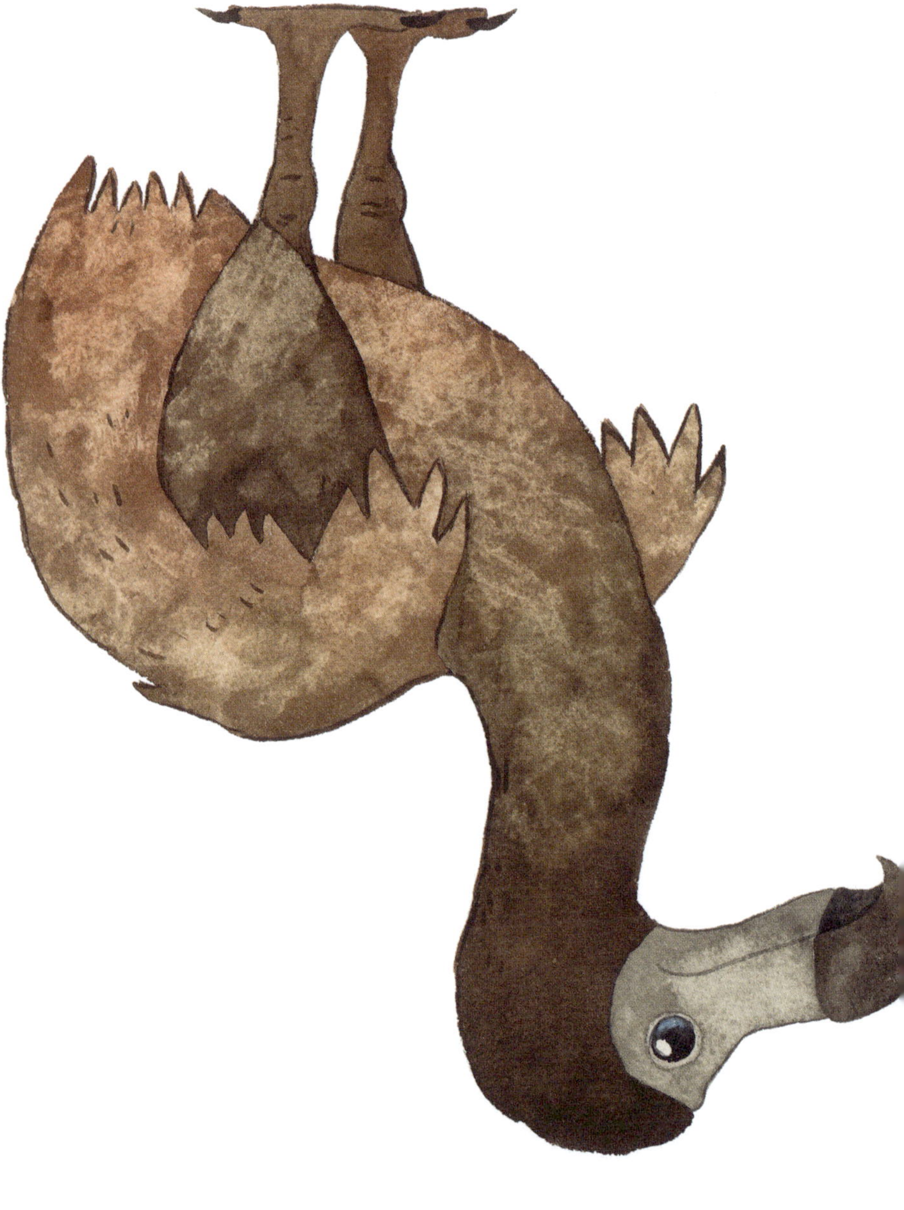

Dead as a dodo

The plight of this poor bird is well known, having been wiped out from Mauritius, their island in the Indian Ocean, by Portuguese explorers in the seventeenth century. Being so easy to catch, their name means stupid. It must have been like shooting turkey burgers in a freezer. They live on in our language, though, as a reference to something that is no longer popular. Think 'skinny jeans are as dead as a dodo', 'floppy disks…', 'boy bands…' etc. etc.

Don't count your chickens

People have been warning about chickens and future plans since this saying was first recorded in a 2,500-year-old Aesop fable. Just because your hens and rooster seem to be getting on, doesn't mean all the eggs they have laid will produce chicks – some will definitely be yolkers. For most things in life, it's best not to presume too much, as that may turn around and bite you on the arse!

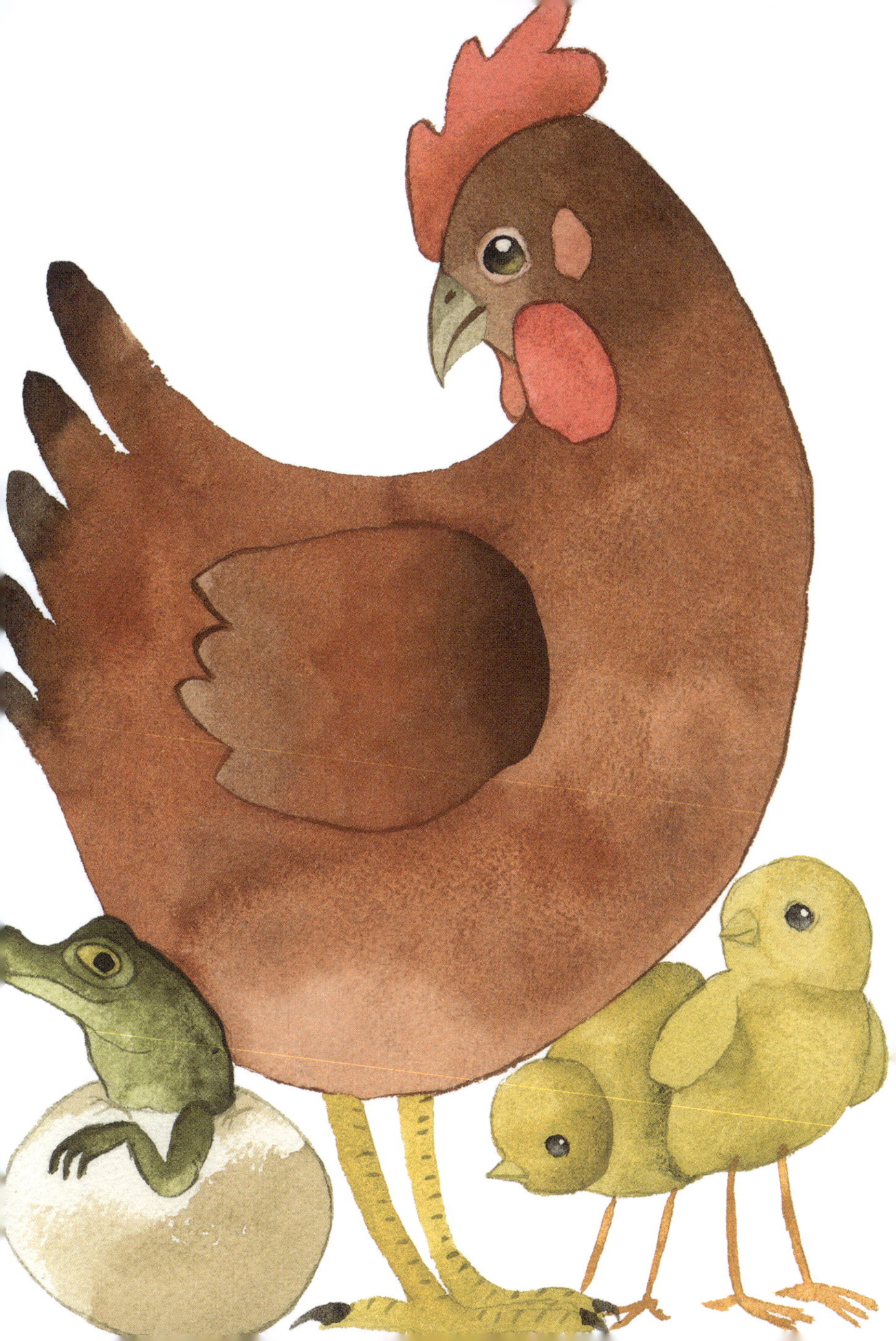

Dovetail

Let's talk business. To 'dovetail' in one's profession, AKA to move easily and securely from one role to another, is a phrase that comes from carpentry. Specifically the dovetail joint, a joinery method that utilises the tapered design of the dove's tail feathers to create an easy and steadfast bond. The phrase has apparently been in use since the 1600s, but woodwork goes as far back as the ancient Egyptians.

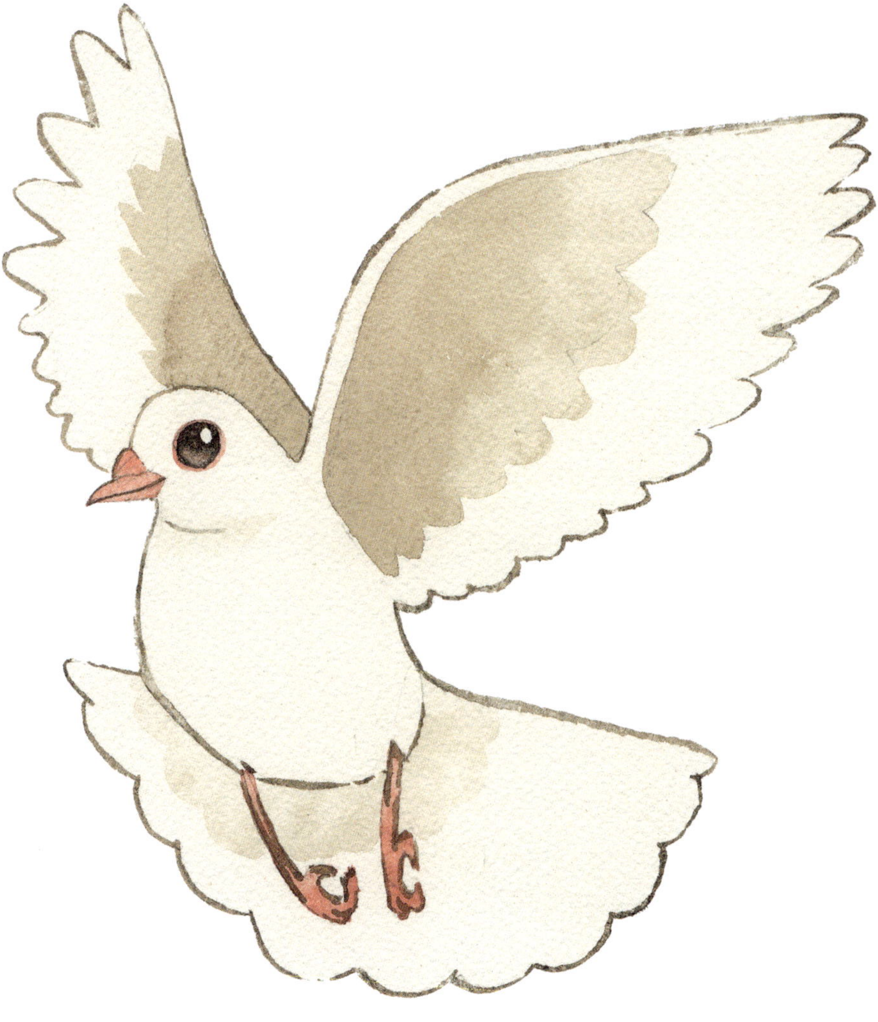

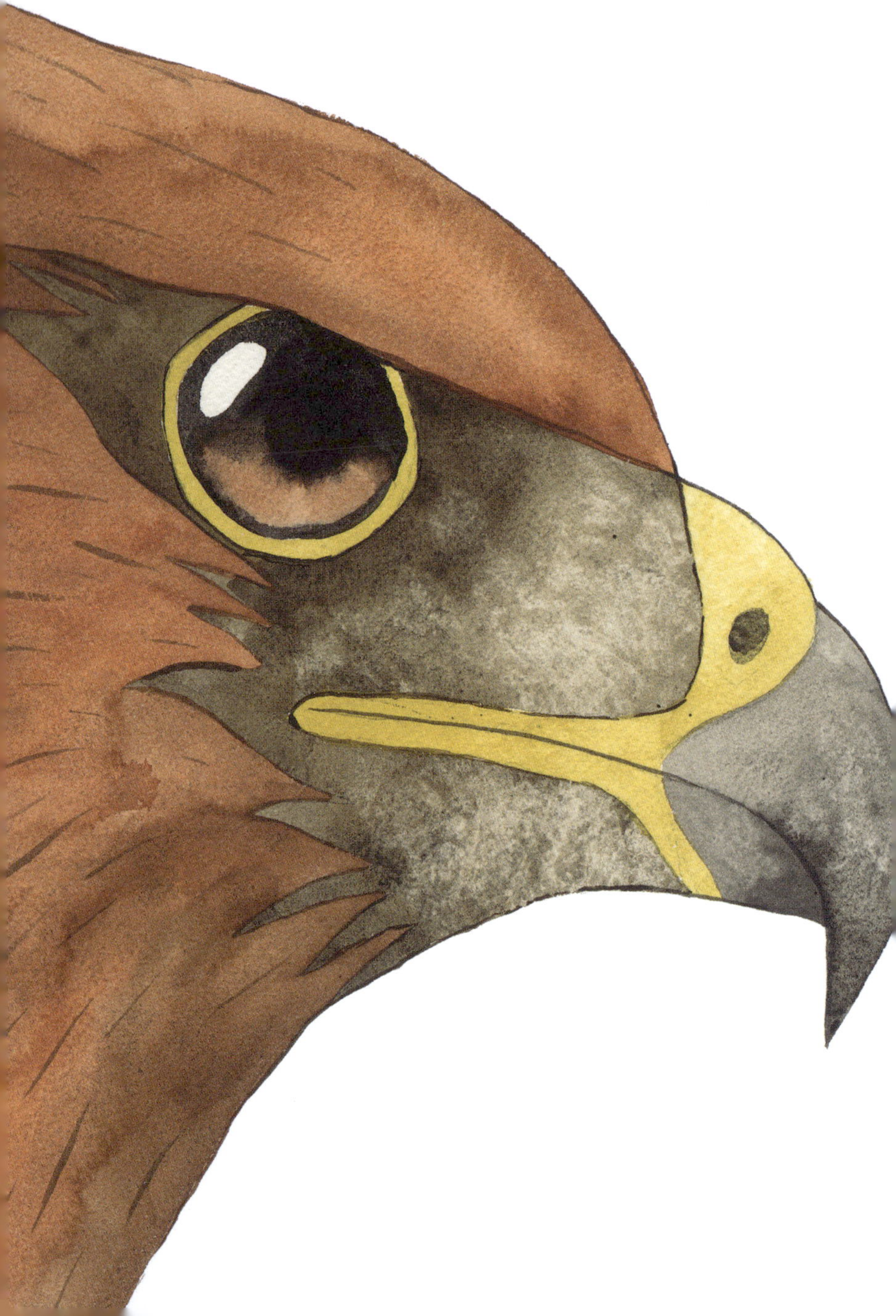

Eagle-eyed

An eagle's colossal wingspan or powerful beak and talons aren't even its most vital weapons – instead, its razor-sharp eyes are its greatest asset. Said to be actually bigger than their brain, an eagle's peepers are essential for the king of birds. Eight times sharper than a human's and able to spot their prey up to 2 miles away, it's no wonder someone who can perceive a situation with clarity is likened to an eagle.

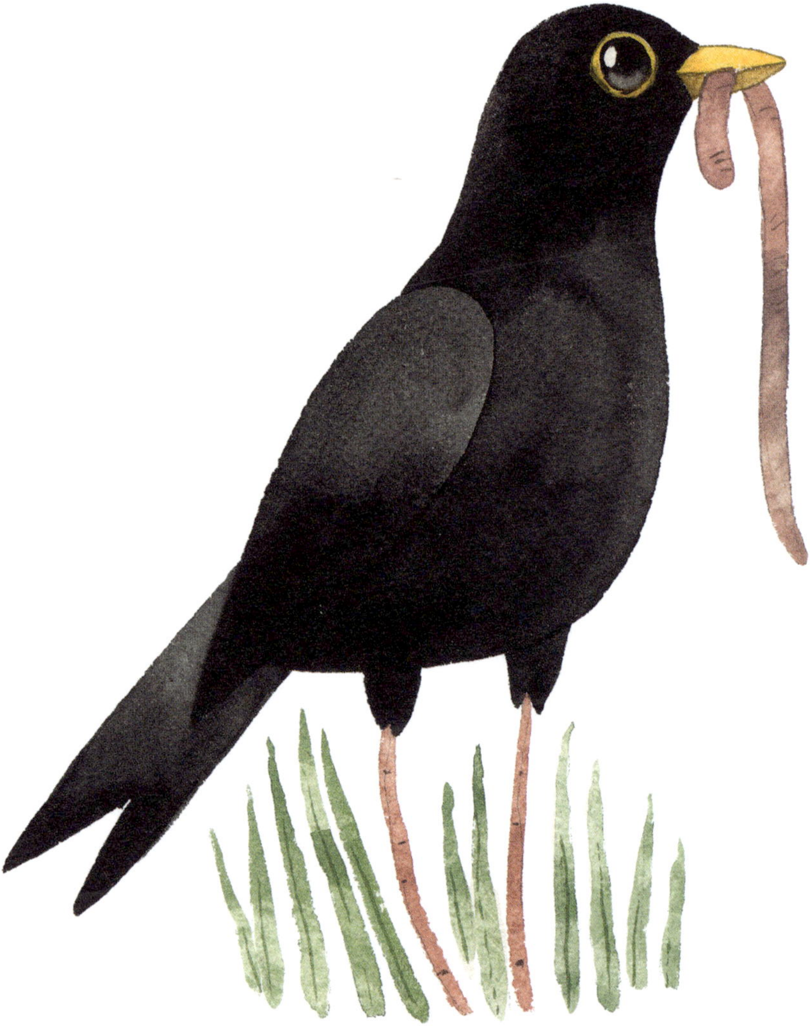

The early bird catches the worm

Round my way, the earliest risers for the dawn chorus are usually the blackbirds, singing with gusto. They're up and making the most of those early, productive hours rather than pressing snooze and going back to sleep. People have been trying to succeed by being the 'early bird' since the saying was first recorded in print in the 1600s, but unfortunately it's not always as easy as people say. Zzzz.

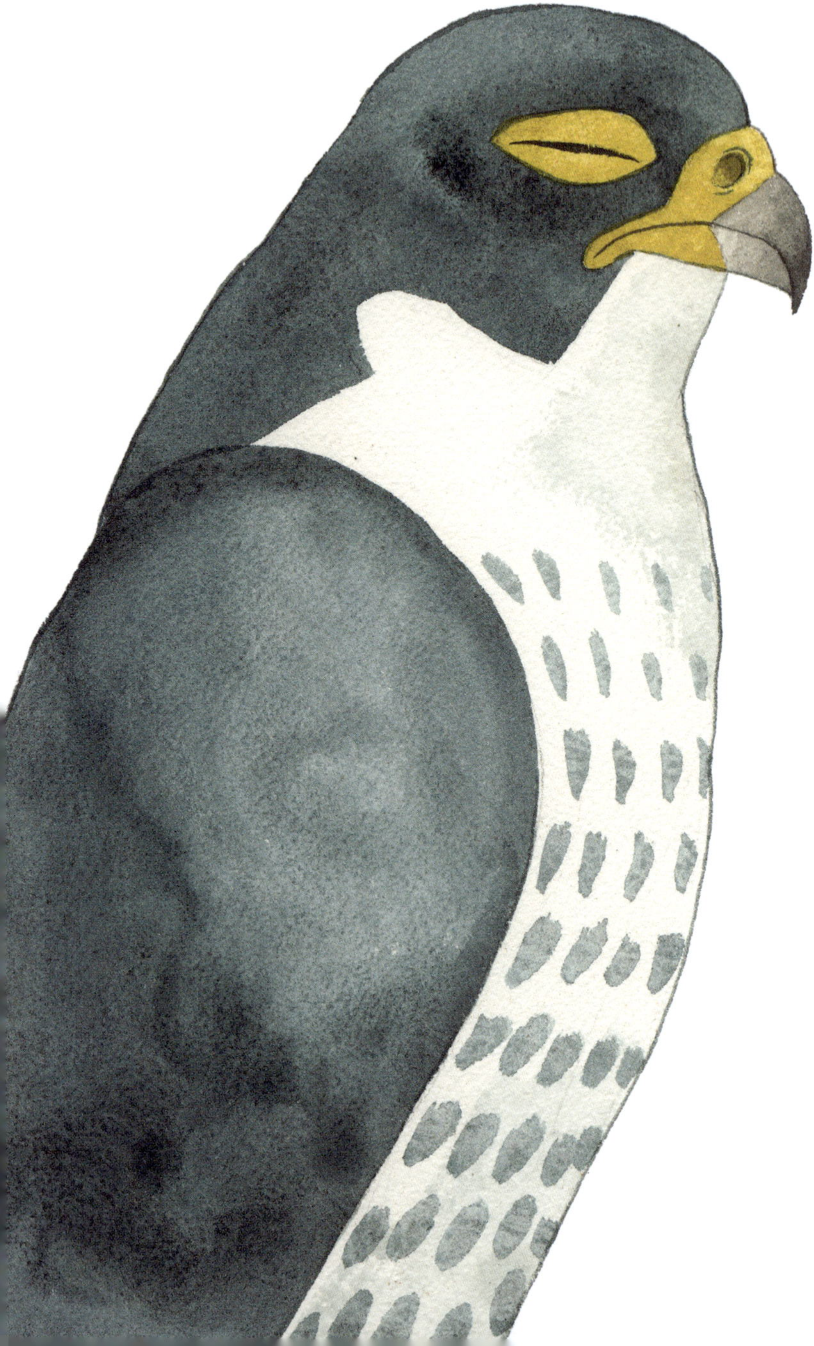

Fed up

Falcons and hawks are very particular – if they have been fed and they're full then they simply won't hunt. They will happily sit there all day not budging. Just like us, when we have reached our limit and enough is enough.

For the birds

Meaning scrap, trivial, inconsequential, and also a polite way for a person in society to call something out as being horseshit. In the Victorian era, horses were vital and the cobbled streets would have been lined with manure. The hayseeds found within the dung were perfect for the resident city-dwelling birds to pick over and feast upon. So don't worry about that, it's for the birds.

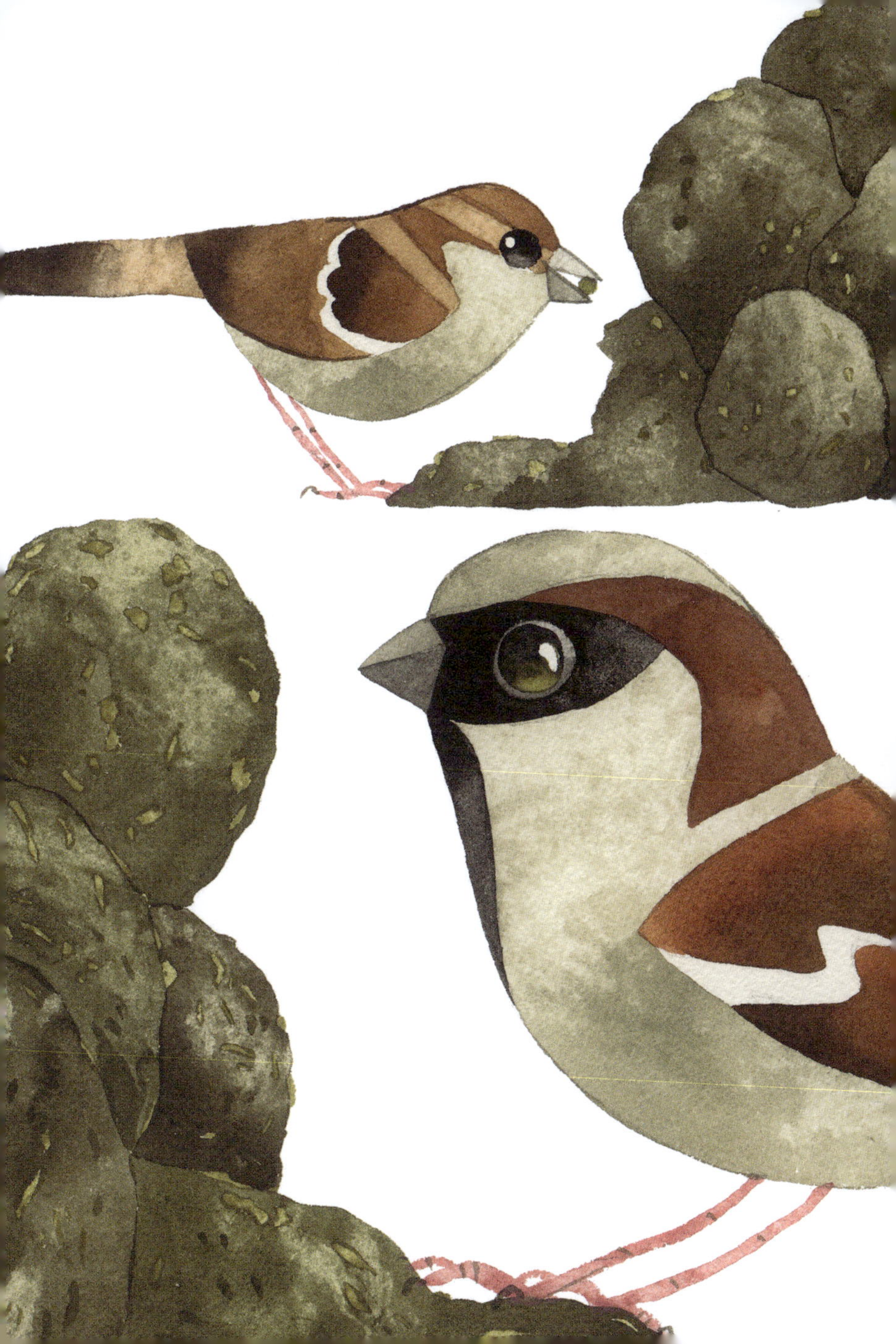

Get your ducks in a row

One of the most joyful sights in nature is that of a mother duck leading her ducklings in regimented file from nest to water, snaking round obstacles with the bumbling cute youngsters all desperate to keep up. It's clear this takes some stressful organising and everything needs to be in place before the journey begins. It's much the same as at home or at work, getting everything sorted before any big event – get your ducks in order first.

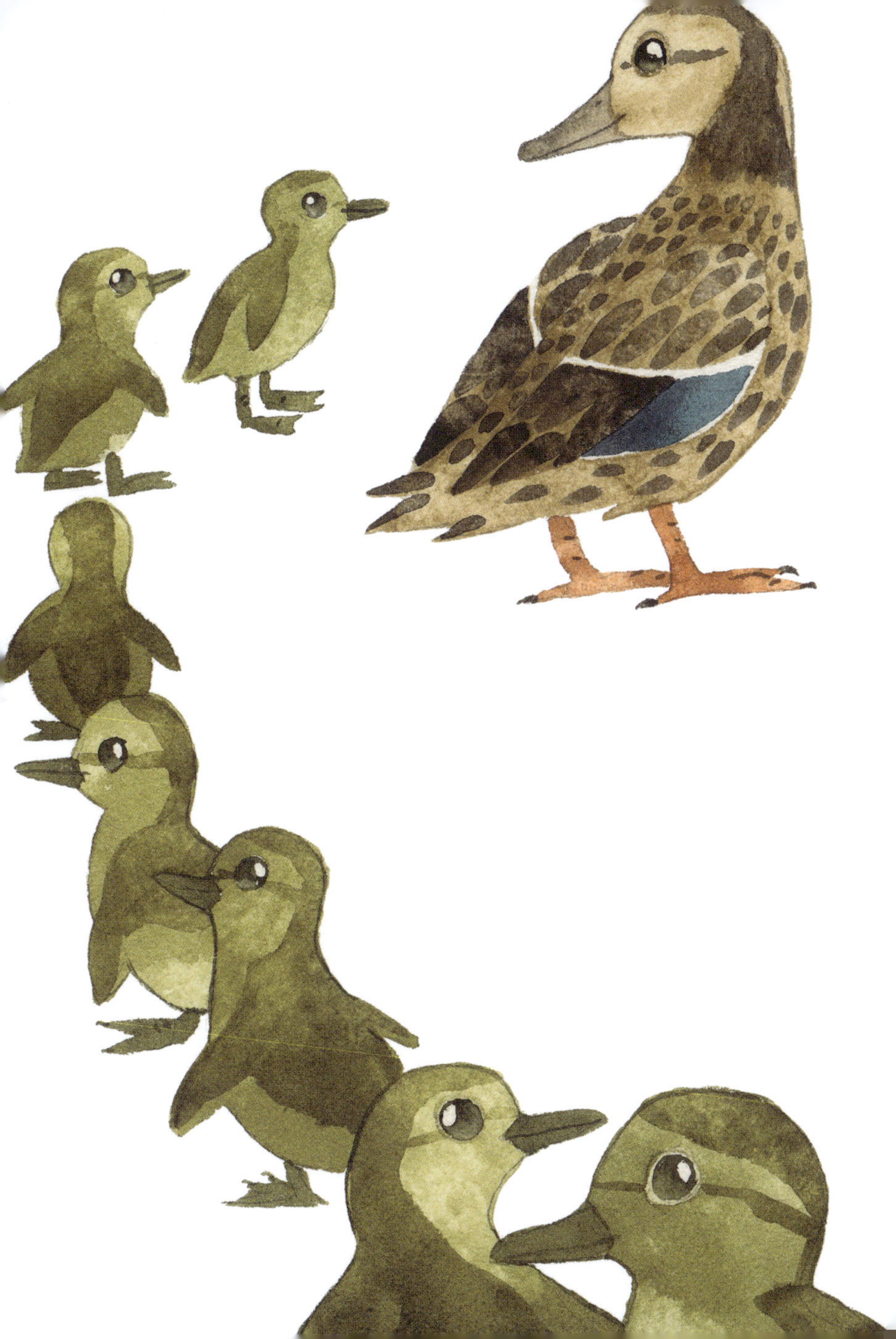

Getting up at sparrow's fart

A beautiful old phrase from northern England, meaning early in the morning. So offensively early that nobody else would be up, except for the early-rising sparrows. It's these still, silent mornings that are so quiet you can hear a sparrow fart.

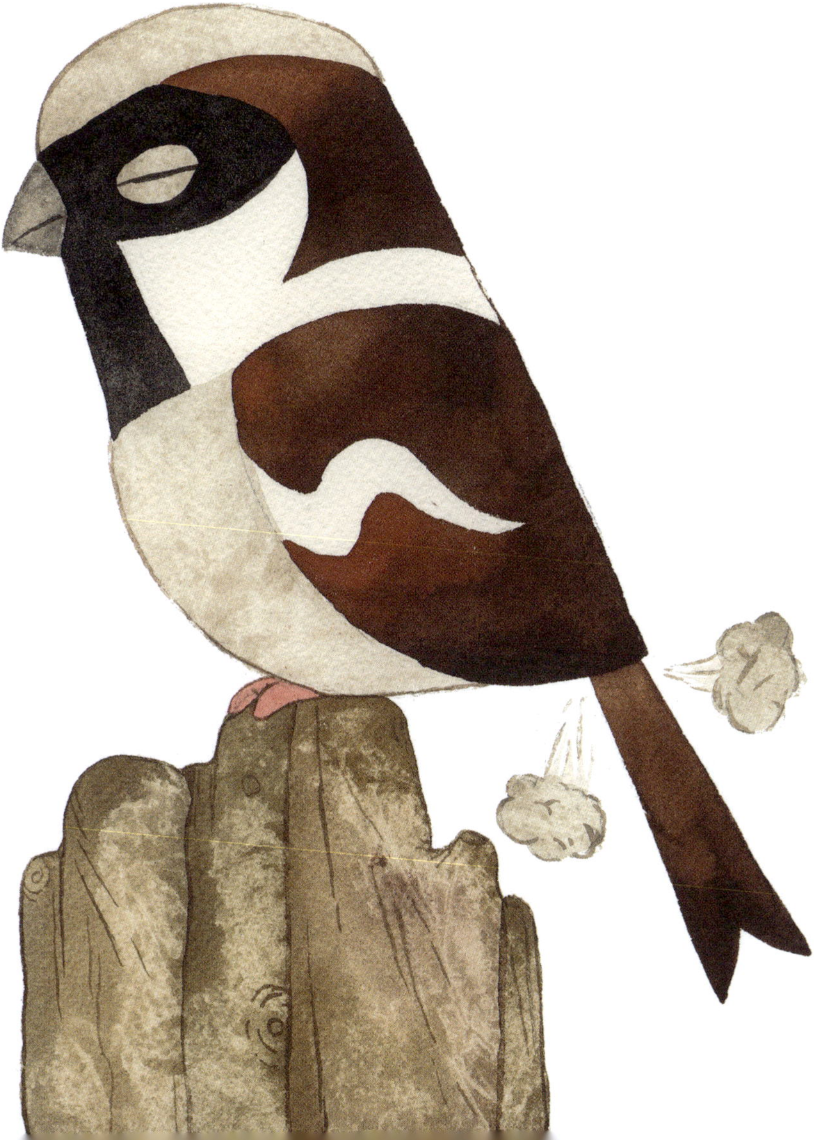

Ghetto bird

We've all seen enough Hollywood movies to know how powerful and intimidating US police helicopters appear. During the 1990s they were seen so frequently in certain neighbourhoods that they became known as 'ghetto birds'. Unfortunately, it was also seen as a bullying and aggressive tactic that was a violation of people's privacy.

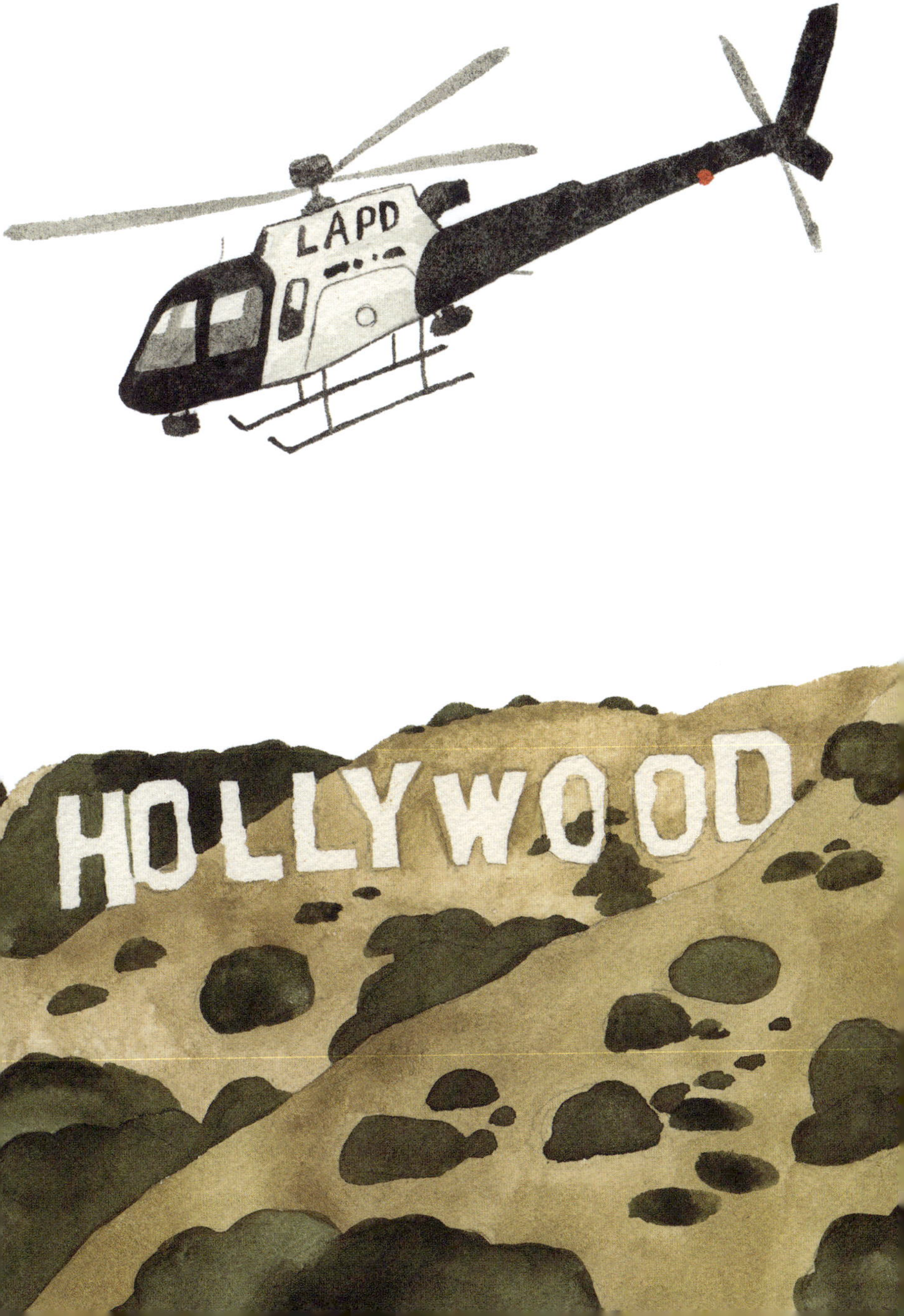
LAPD
HOLLYWOOD

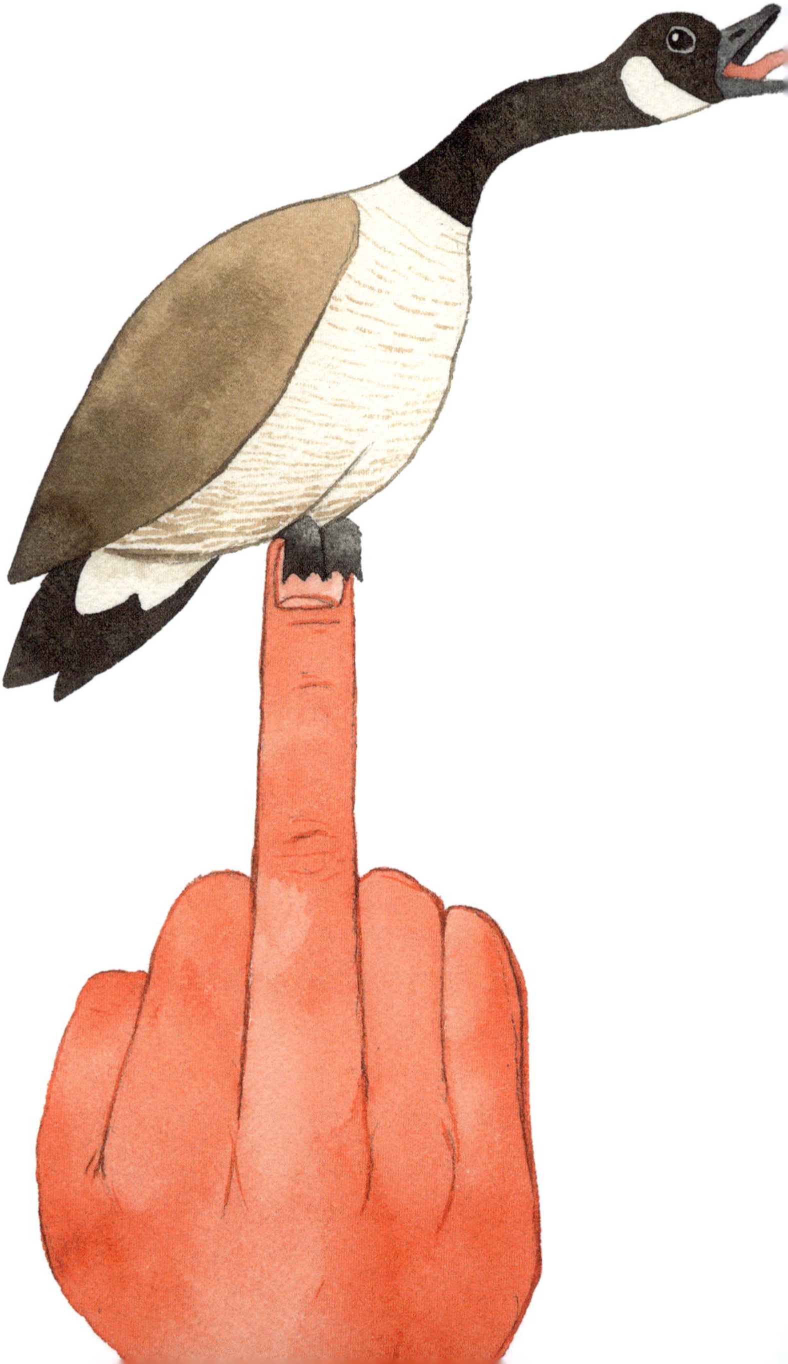

Giving the bird

The sticking up of one's middle finger has been seen as an obscene act since the ancient Greeks were flipping the bird at each other in their togas. This phrase only really came about in the 1920s, when in riotous vaudeville theaters in the US, audience members would express their disdain of the acts on stage by hissing like geese whilst making the hand gesture.

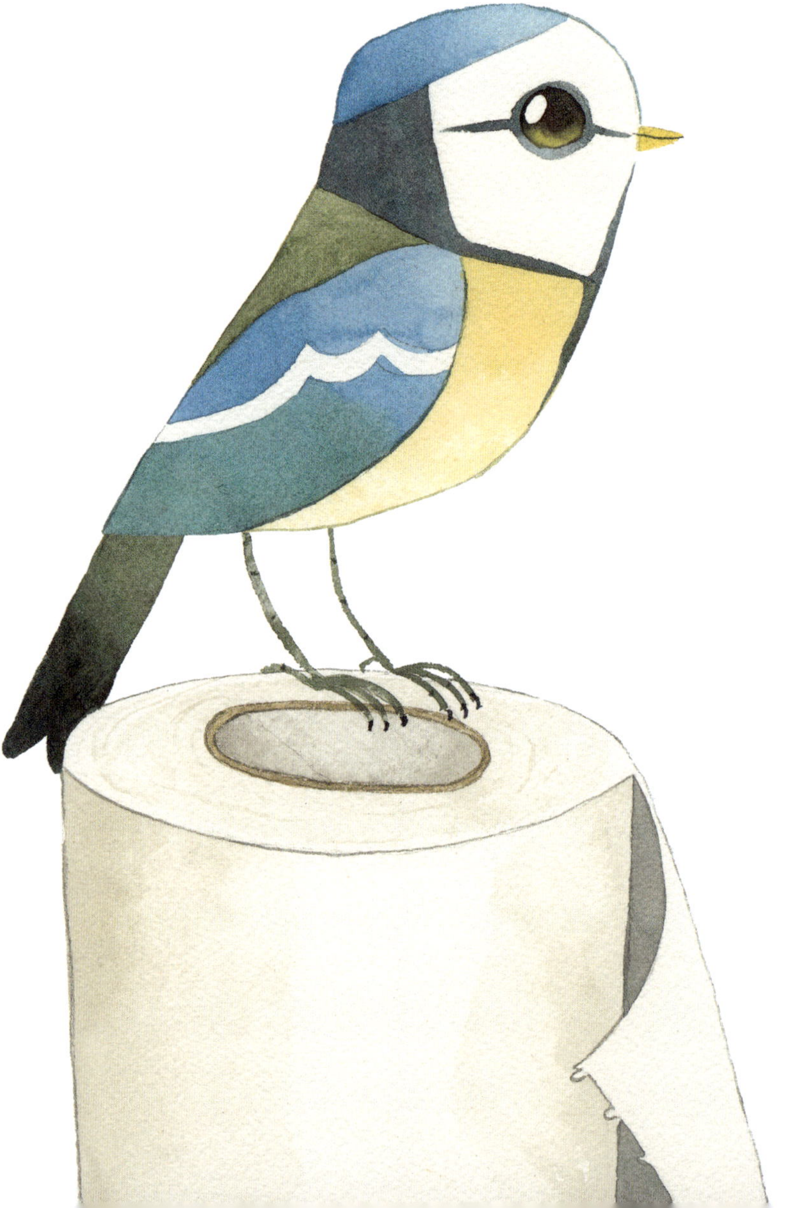

Going for a tomtit

Pony, rabbit and dog are some other animal stars of Cockney rhyming slang. But what is a tomtit? Colloquially birds have had different names around the country, and in the east end of London the charming blue tit would have been known as a tomtit. I'm sure we can all guess the activity alluded to by this pearl of a phrase.

Guttersnipe

A Dickensian street urchin, scrabbling through rubbish on the street like a wading snipe. The mottled brown bird forages for morsels on estuaries and riversides. It would have been commonly observed on the detritus-strewn banks of the Thames, browsing, probing, turning over stones and foraging for food.

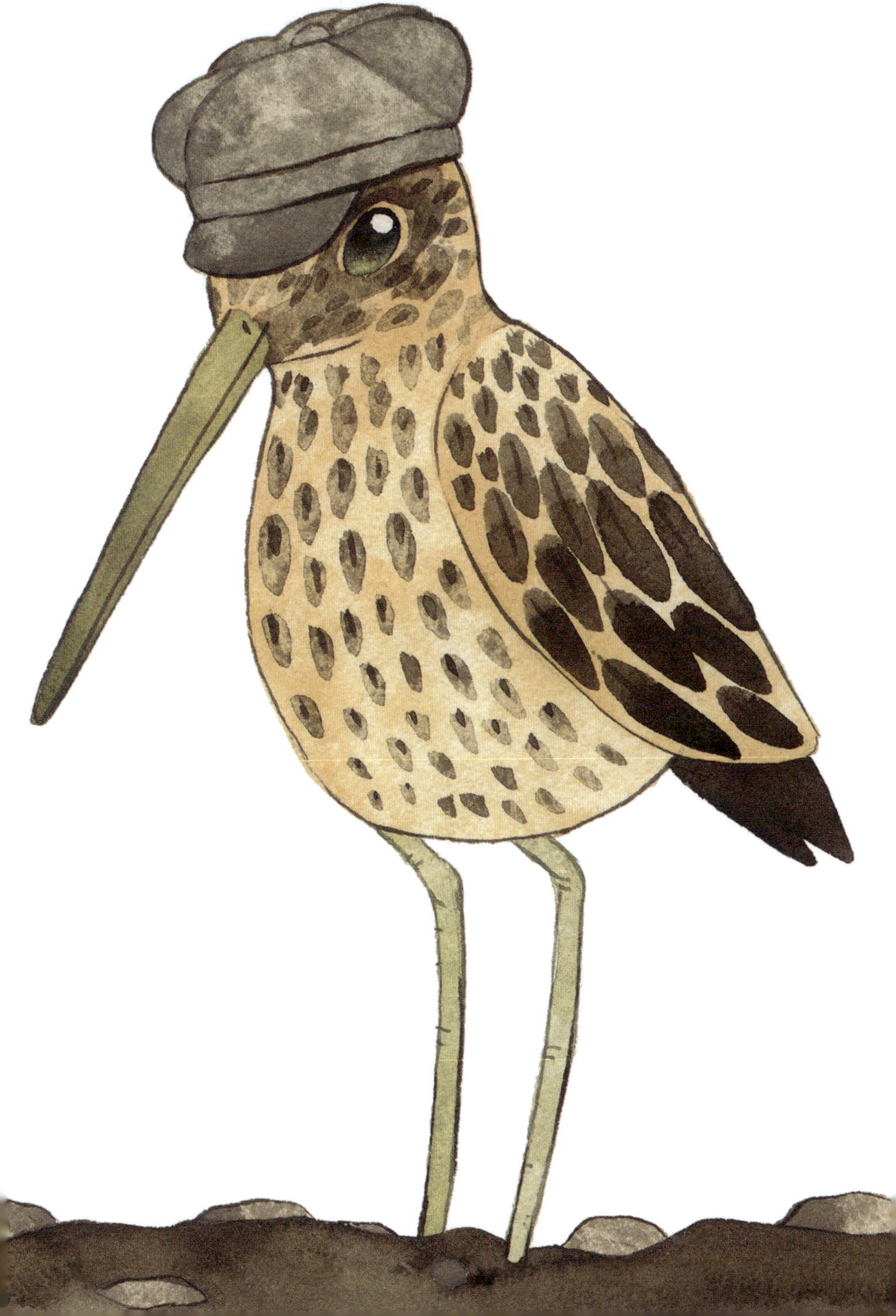

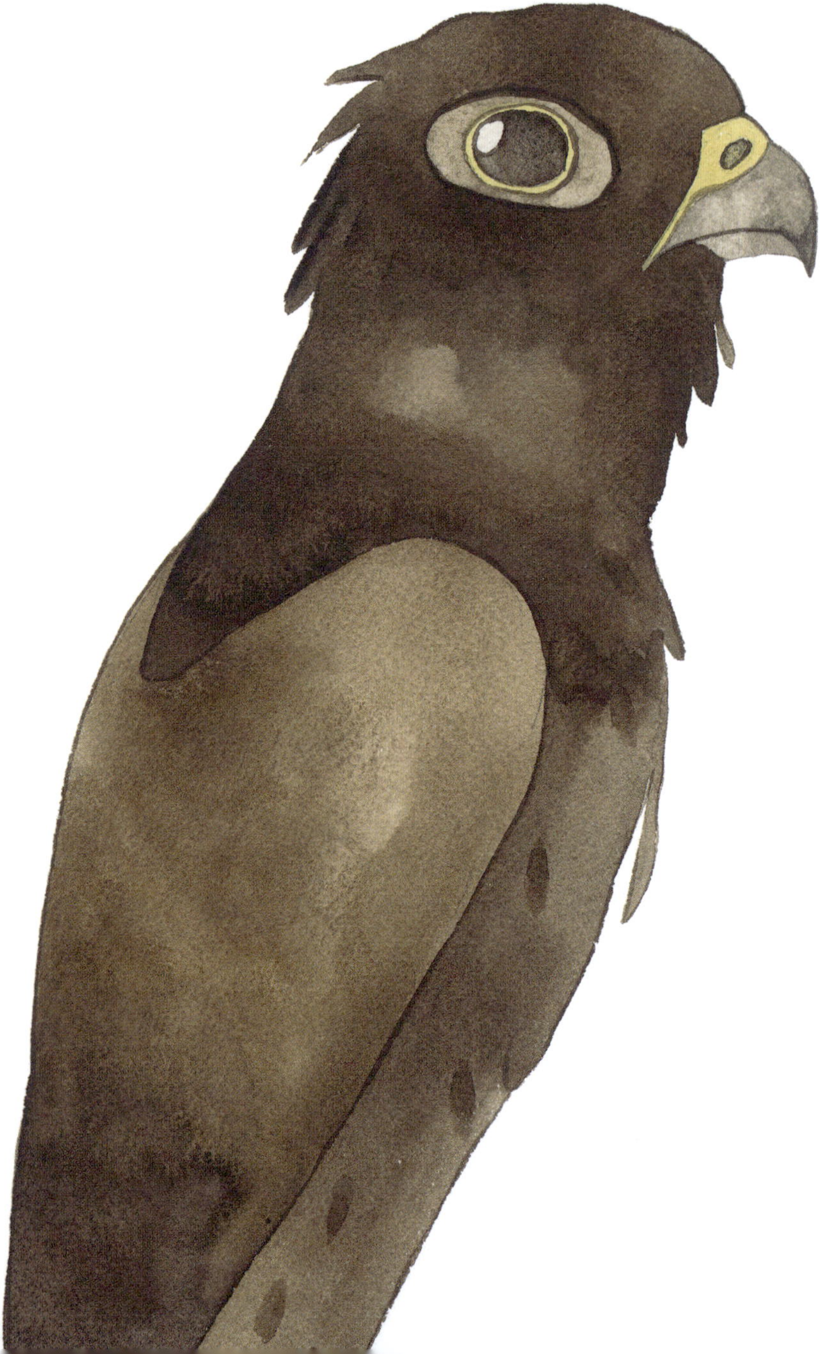

Haggard

Been out all night, a bit tired and not quite looking your best? Feeling haggard? This expression originates from the 1560s, used to describe a freshly-caught wild hawk, possibly underweight with straggly feathers and a wild, haunted look in its eye.

Halcyon days

When we look back upon a peaceful time in our past, it can be referred to as the 'halcyon days'. This phrase stretches back to Greek mythology, telling of the goddess Alcyone who, transformed into a kingfisher, would lay her eggs during the middle of winter. This is a terrible time for a bird to nest, but luckily Zeus would grant her a spell of fine and peaceful weather in which to raise her brood.

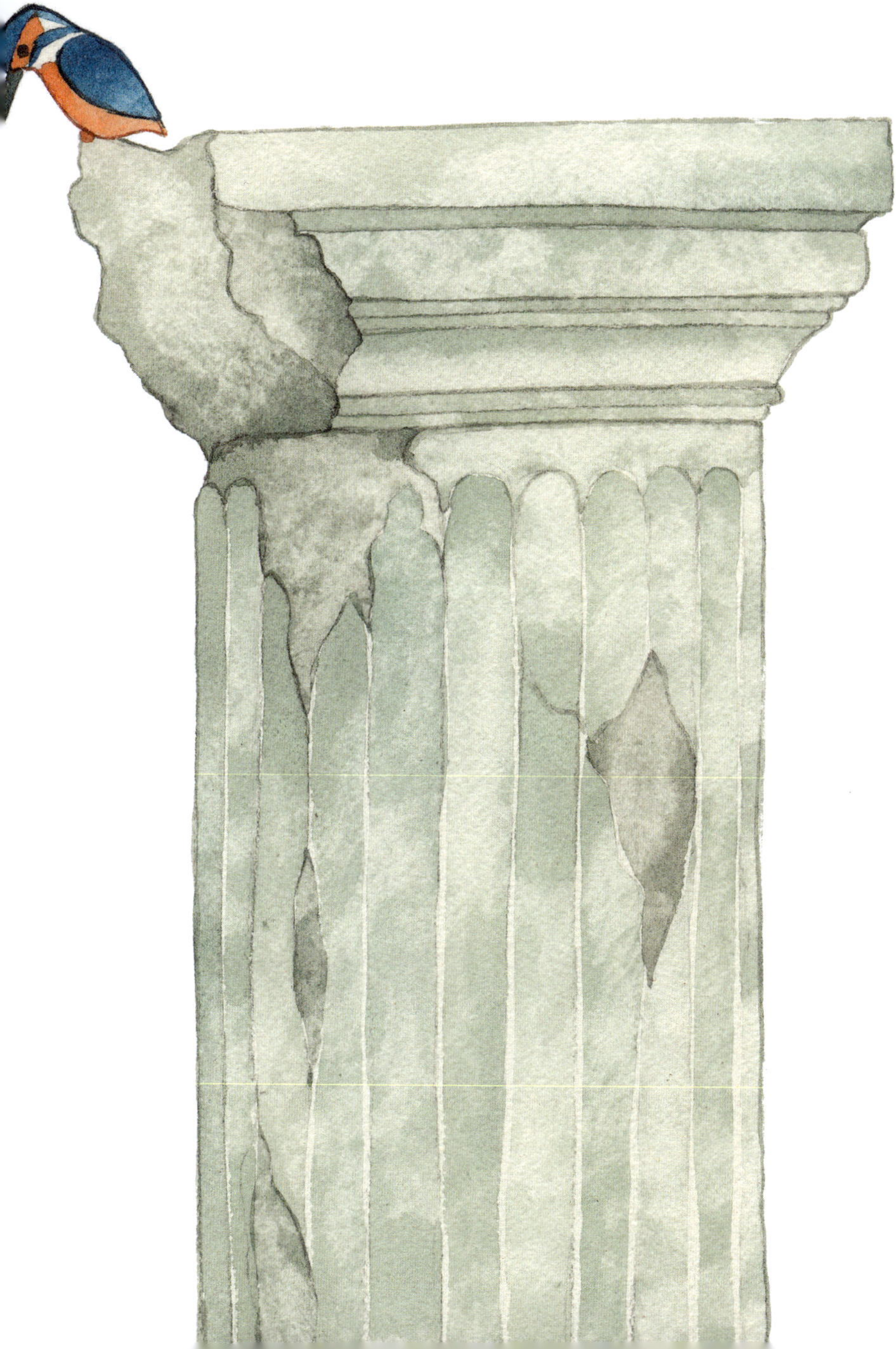

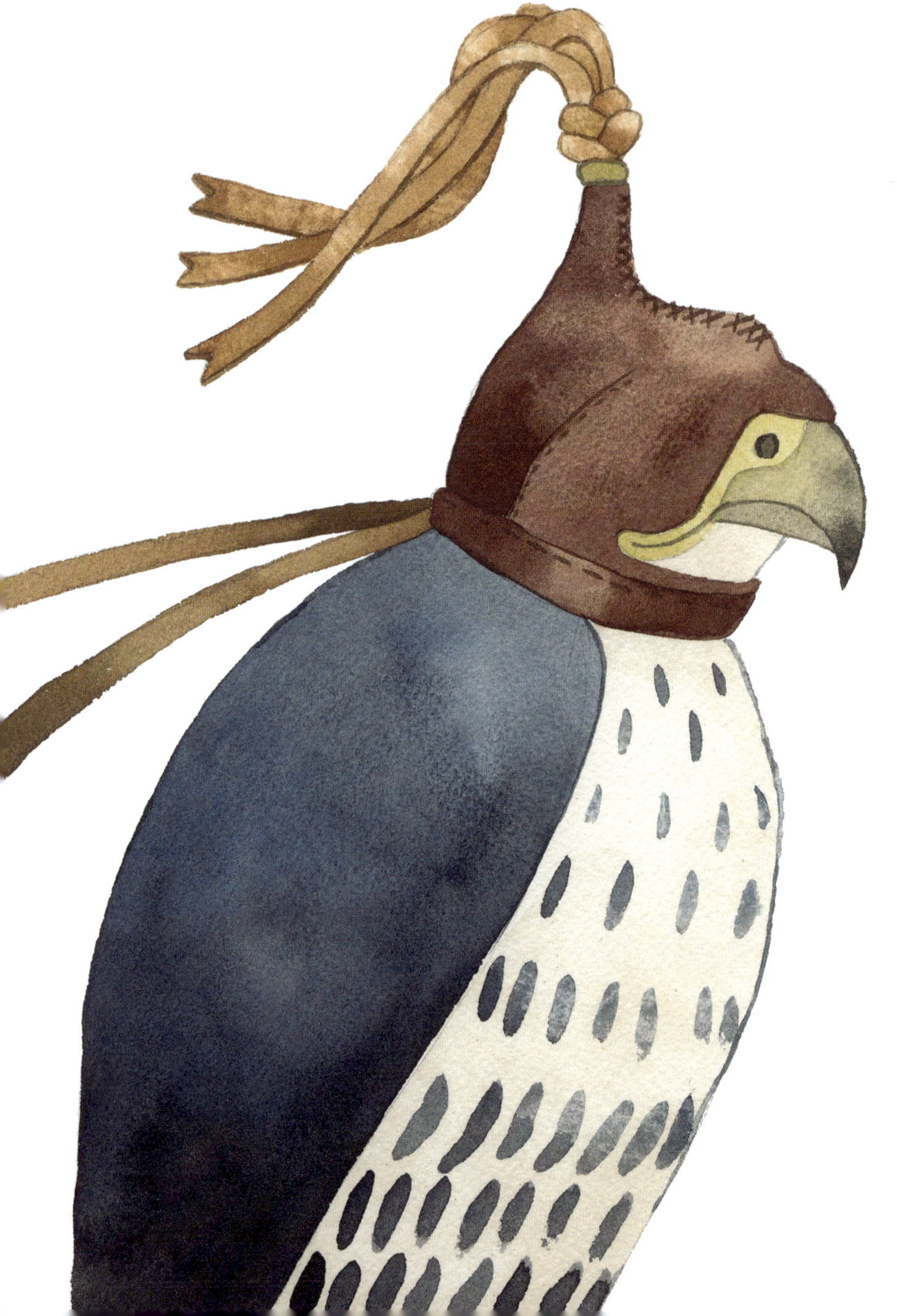

Hoodwinked

Now you have seen the illustration and seen the title, you may actually feel hoodwinked yourself for not realising that this phrase originates from the sixteenth century. It simply means to place a hood on a hawk to close its eyes and calm it down. Do you feel deceived? Tricked? You've been hoodwinked.

In one fell swoop

To achieve one's goal with a precise action, like a peregrine falcon dropping in a lightning-quick stoop to strike its pigeon prey so hard and quick that it is killed instantly. Shakespeare popularised this saying in the 1600s, borrowed from an antiquated falconry term constructed of olde English, and it's still just as popular today.

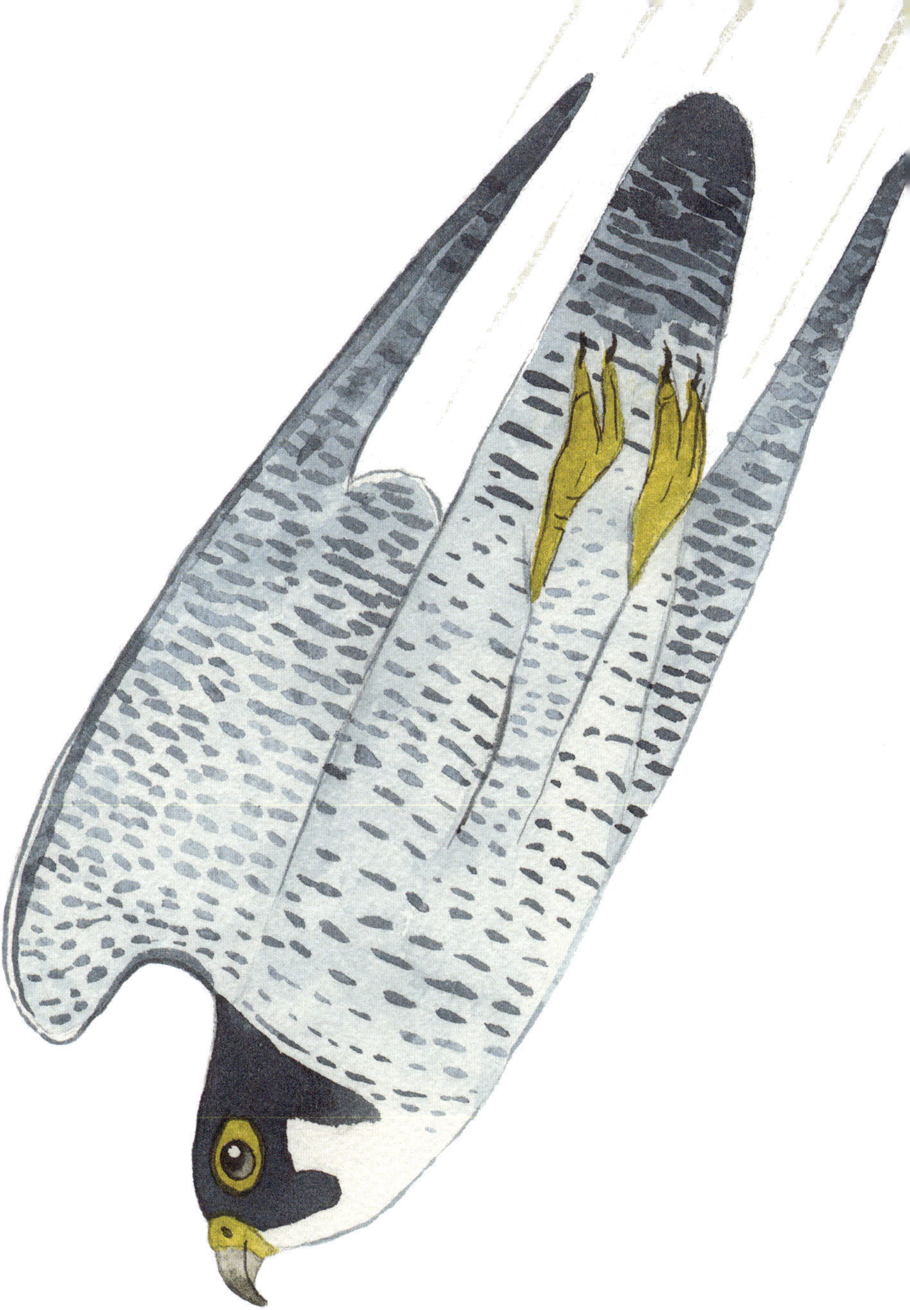

Jailbird

All around the world and for hundreds of years, prisoners, convicts and bad lads have been likened to caged birds, which is quite a winsome and romantic take on someone habitually found in gaol. 'Doing bird' is Cockney rhyming slang from the 1800s referring to bird lime (a sticky substance used to trap birds on branches) and the detainee doing their time or sentence.

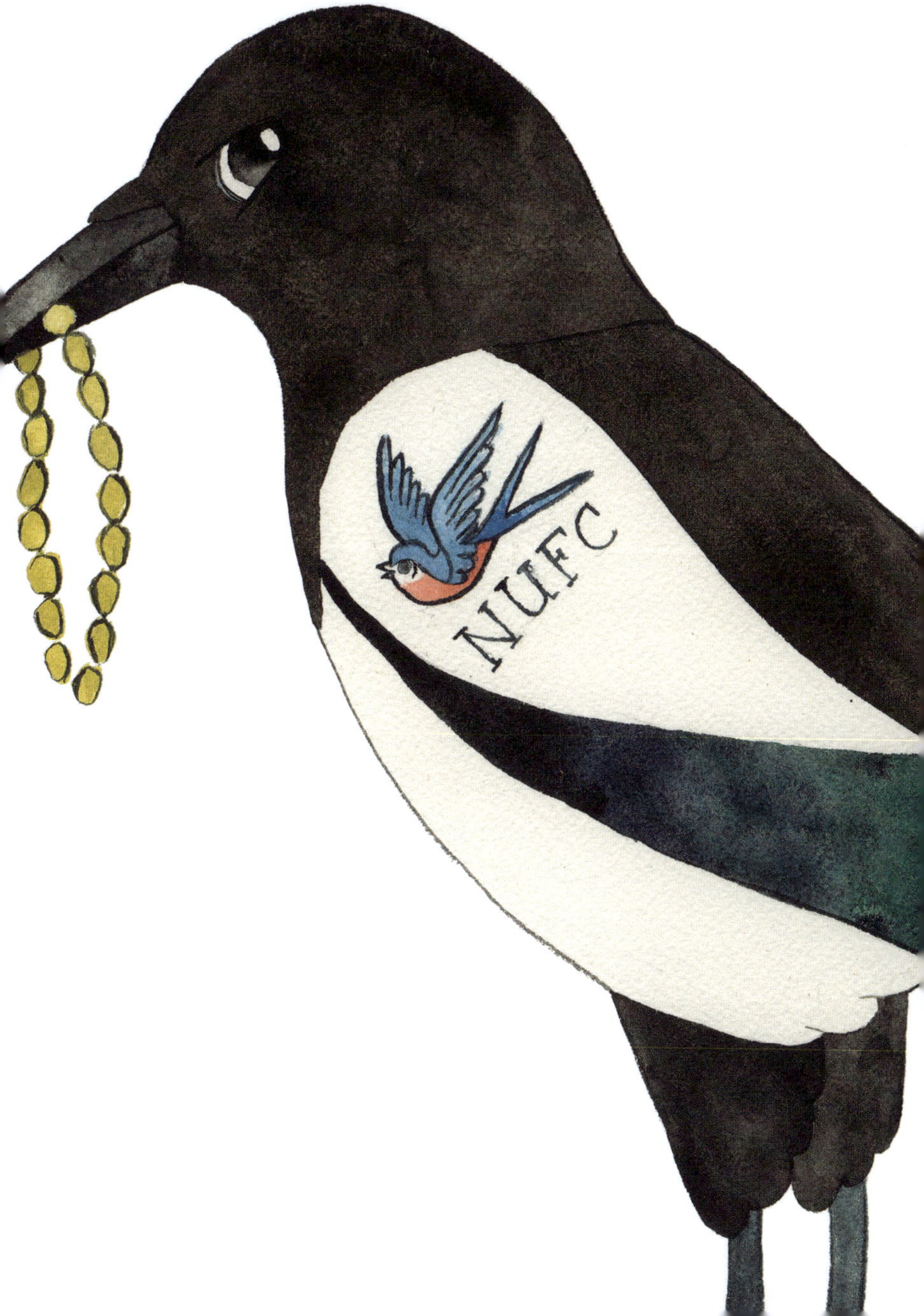
NUFC

Kill two birds with one stone

Who doesn't like to kill two birds with one stone? Not literally, argh! The origin of this phrase is not known, but there's a simple joy from achieving two benefits from one action – like dropping off the kids at school whilst on the way to work or tying your shoelaces whilst bending down to pick up your dog's poo.

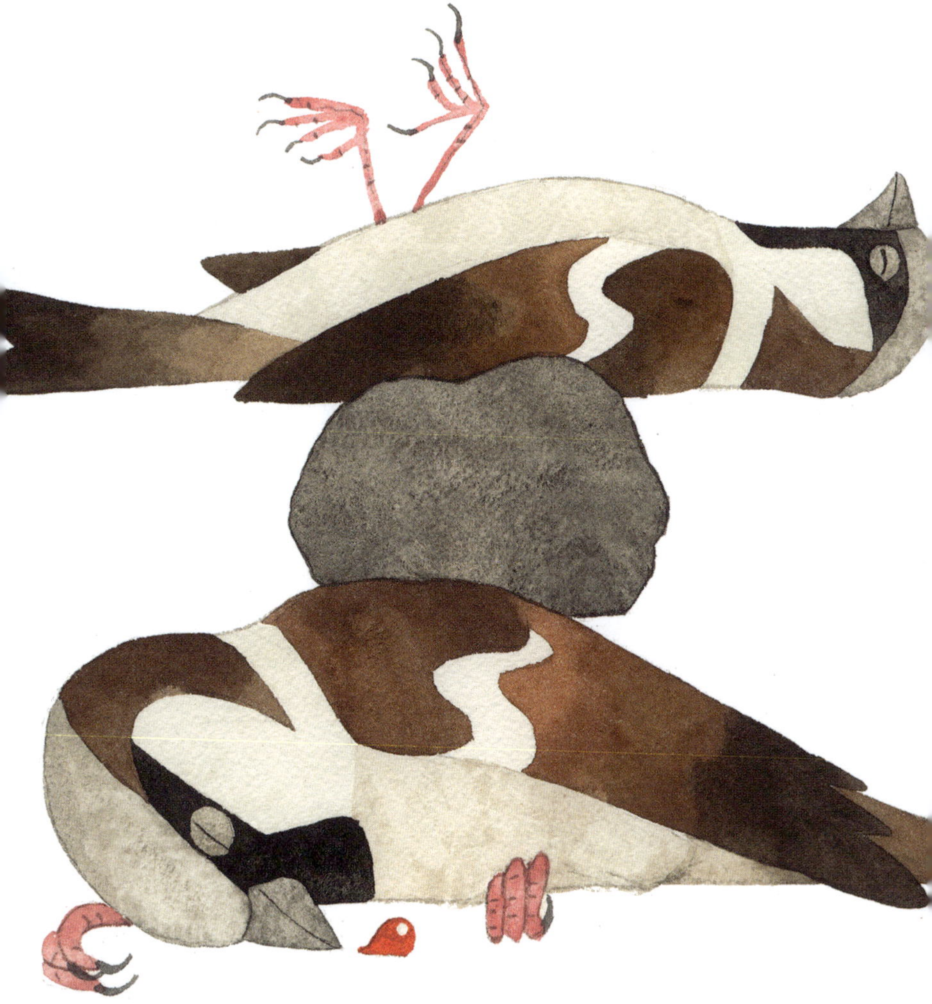

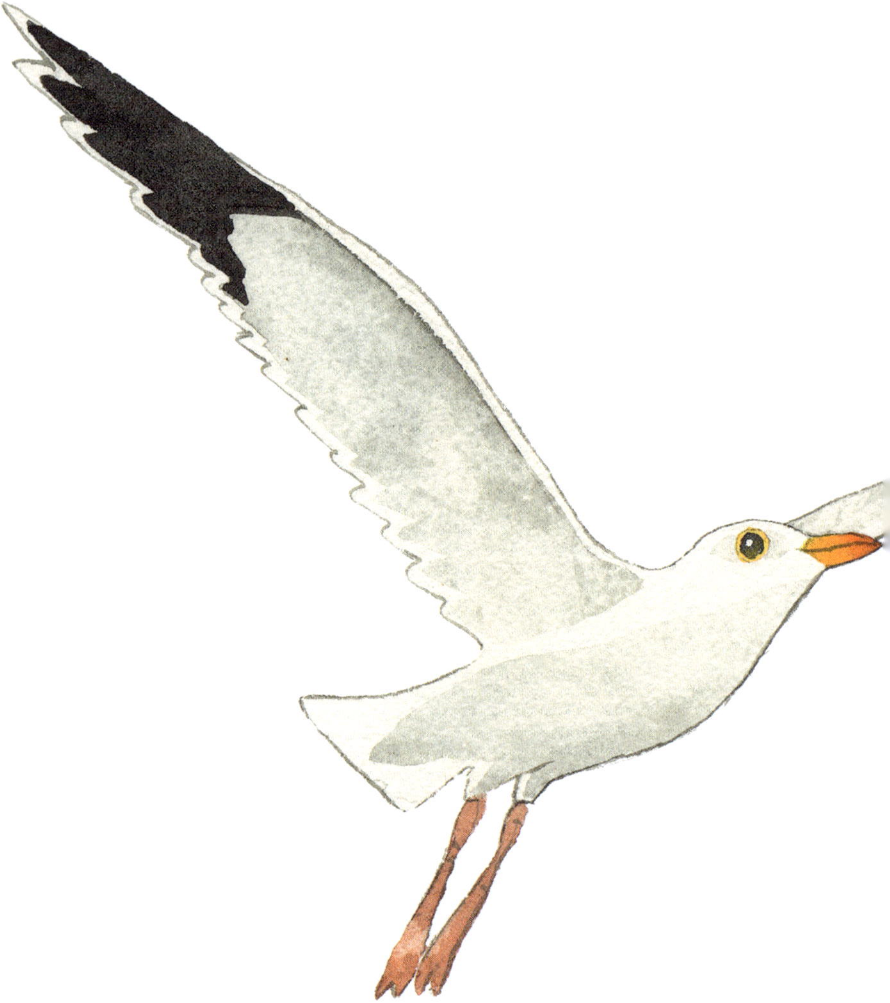

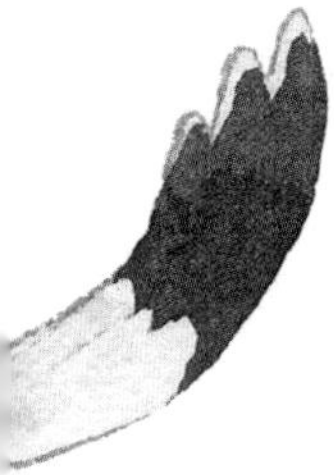

Like a gull takes to the wind

Next time you are enjoying a lovely seaside retreat and you are rather brutishly mugged by a gull for your ice cream, tray of chips or pasty, rather than swearing and shouting why not sit back and watch as the seabird effortlessly glides away with nary a beat of its long elegant wings? So natural and harmoniously in its element.

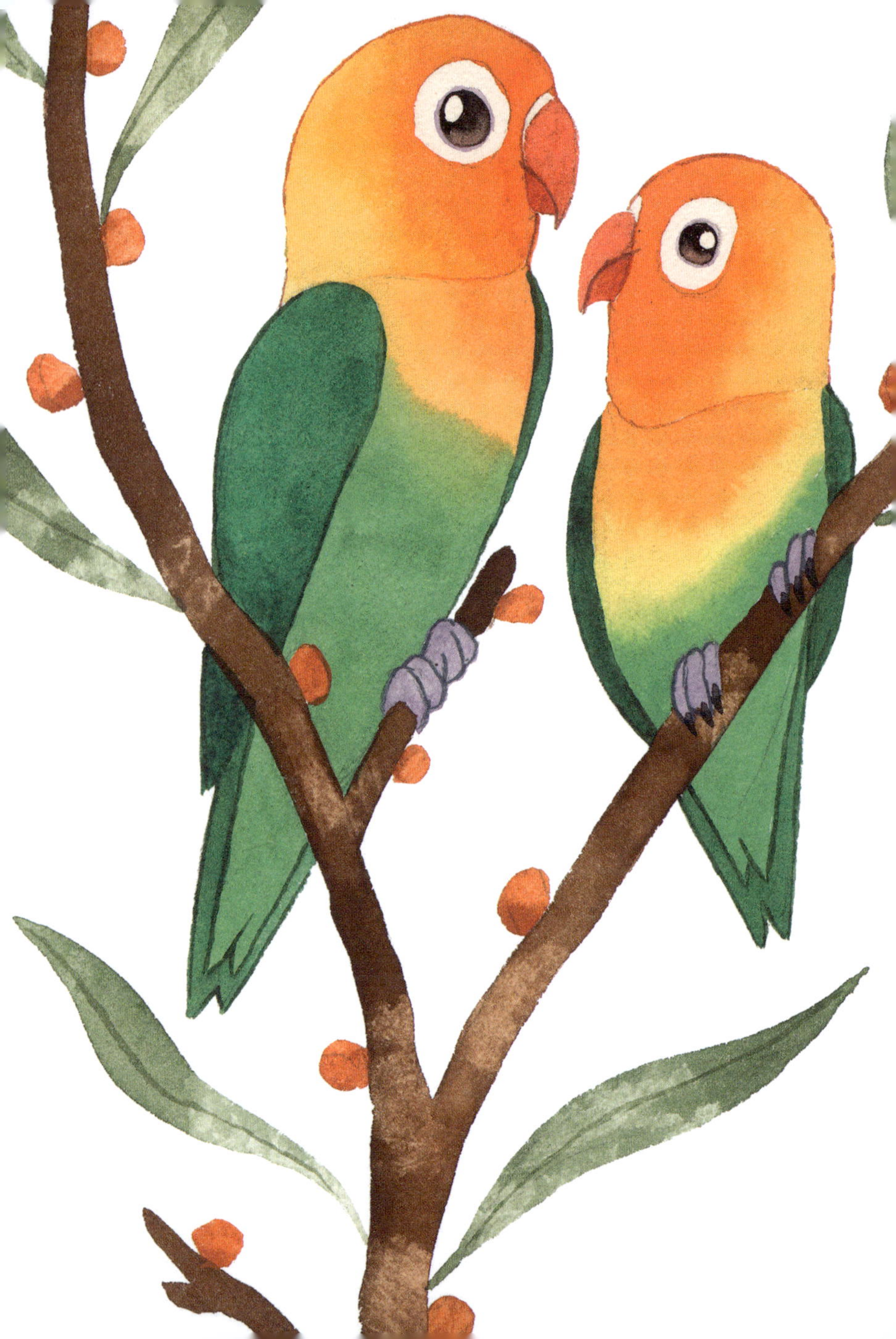

Lovebirds

Like swans, ravens and albatrosses, lovebirds pair for life. None are quite so fond of public displays of affection as these tiny, cute African parrots though – get a room, guys! The birds became popular as pets from the 1700s, and due to their devoted adoration, the expression has radiated into modern parlance.

Night owl

This phrase sprang to life during the Industrial Revolution as society moved away from the circadian rhythms of agriculture and the countryside transformed into a modern, mass-produced technological future. Such urbanisation and economic growth couldn't be accomplished in daylight hours: 24-hour workers and night owls were needed. Unfortunately, inequality, poverty and child labour were side effects of the development.

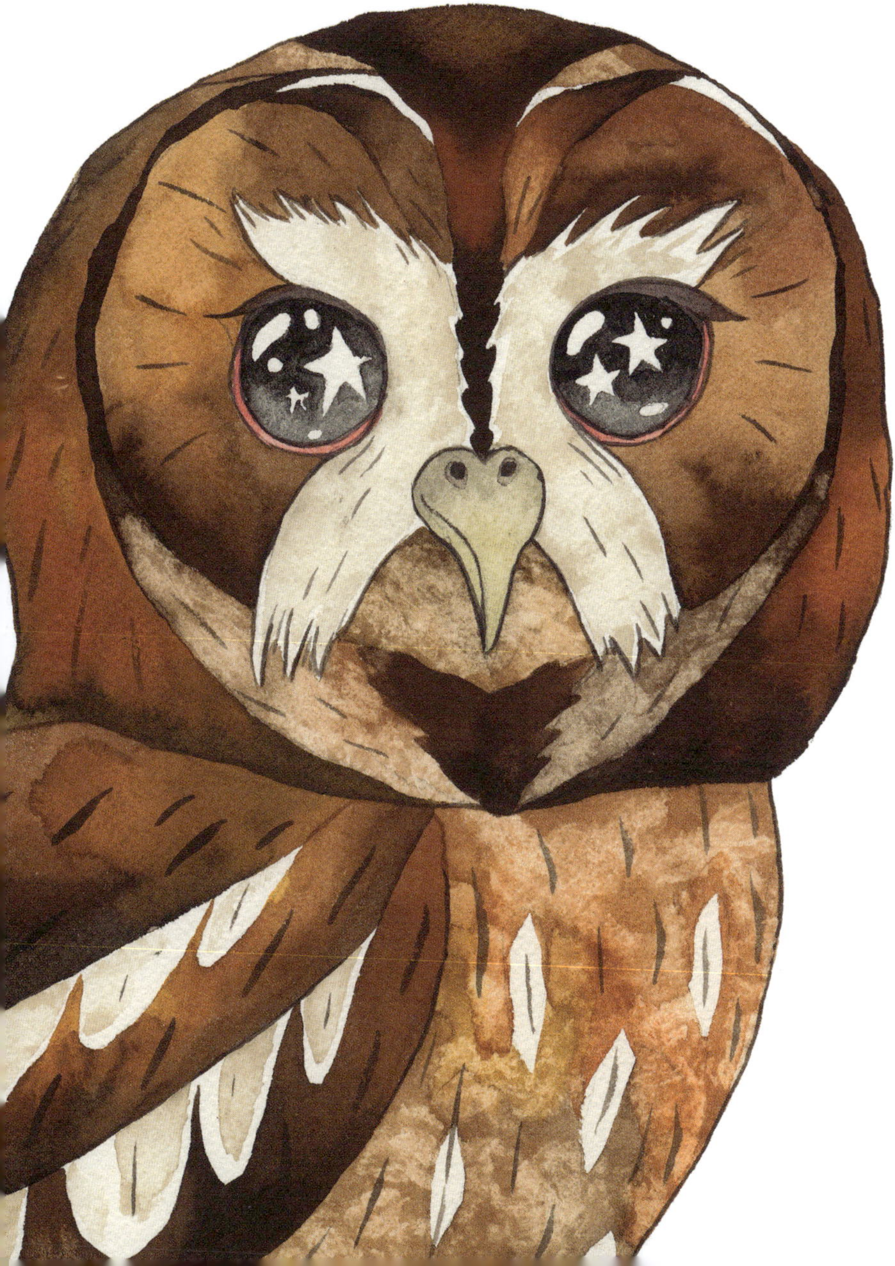

One
swallow
does
not
make
a
summer

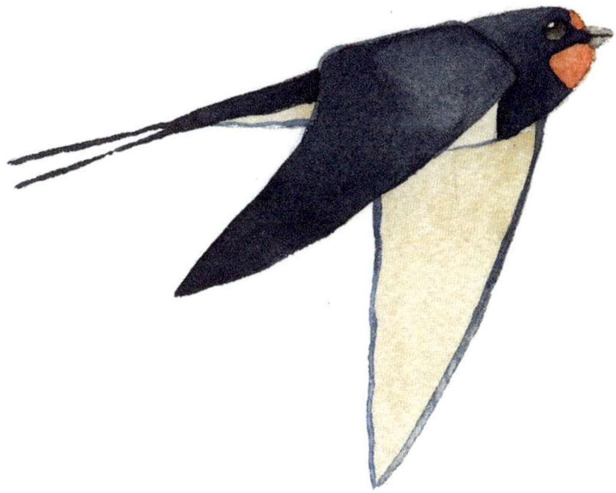

It's true, just as a few warm days doesn't mean it's summer in Britain – it could easily snow the following week. Spotting the first swallow in spring is a thrill, but when they are all back and circling the skies you can be sure summer is just around the corner. We have the Greek philosopher Aristotle to thank for the phrase; he equated spotting the first swallow with being too foolishly hopeful.

Pecking order

Households, schools, friendship groups and workplaces can all have a hidden hierarchy and social structure. Scientific studies from the early twentieth century show poultry also fit this theory, with chickens only pecking others lower in the hierarchy; in effect punching down. I can testify to this – I used to feed chickens as a child and they formed an orderly queue to peck me.

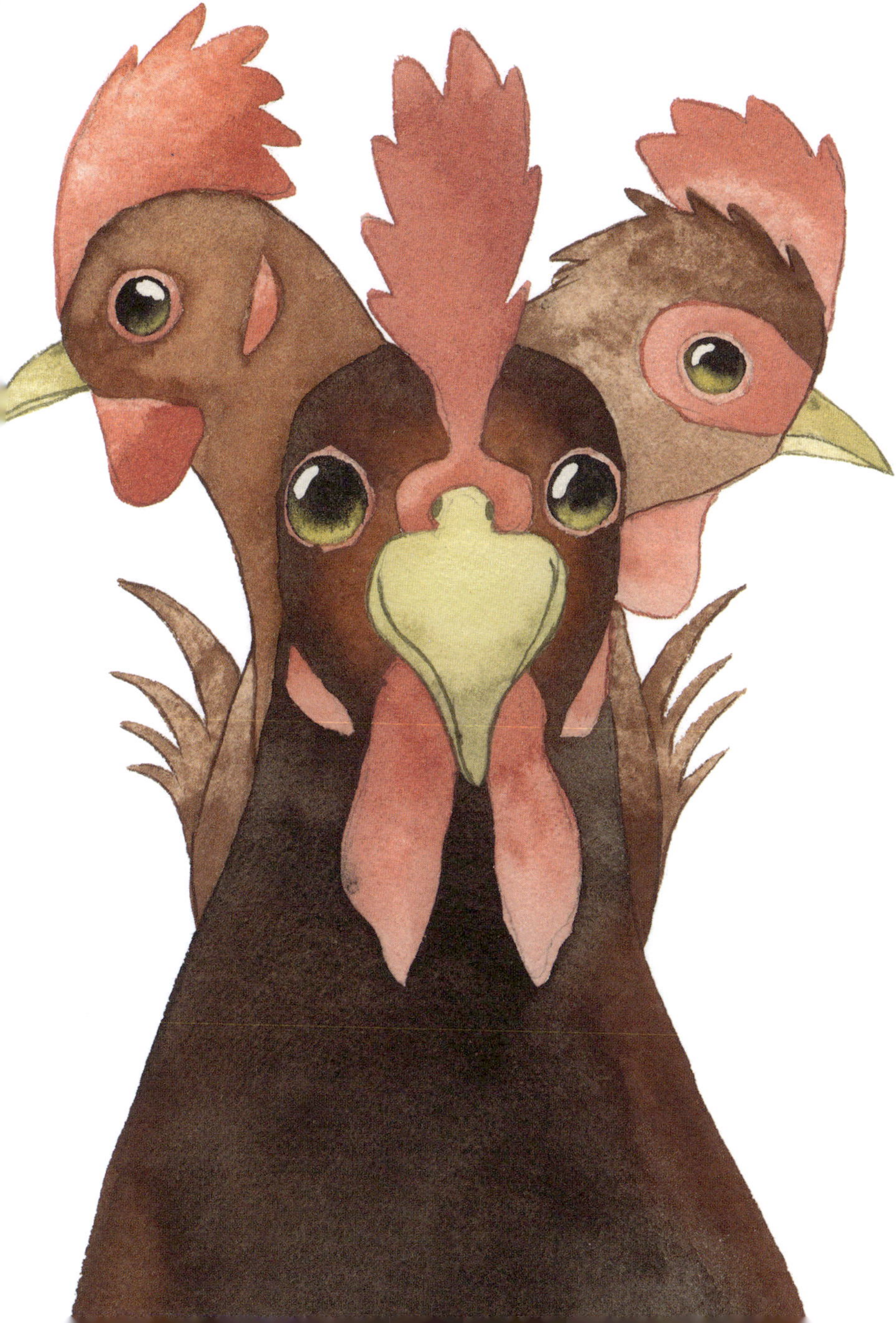

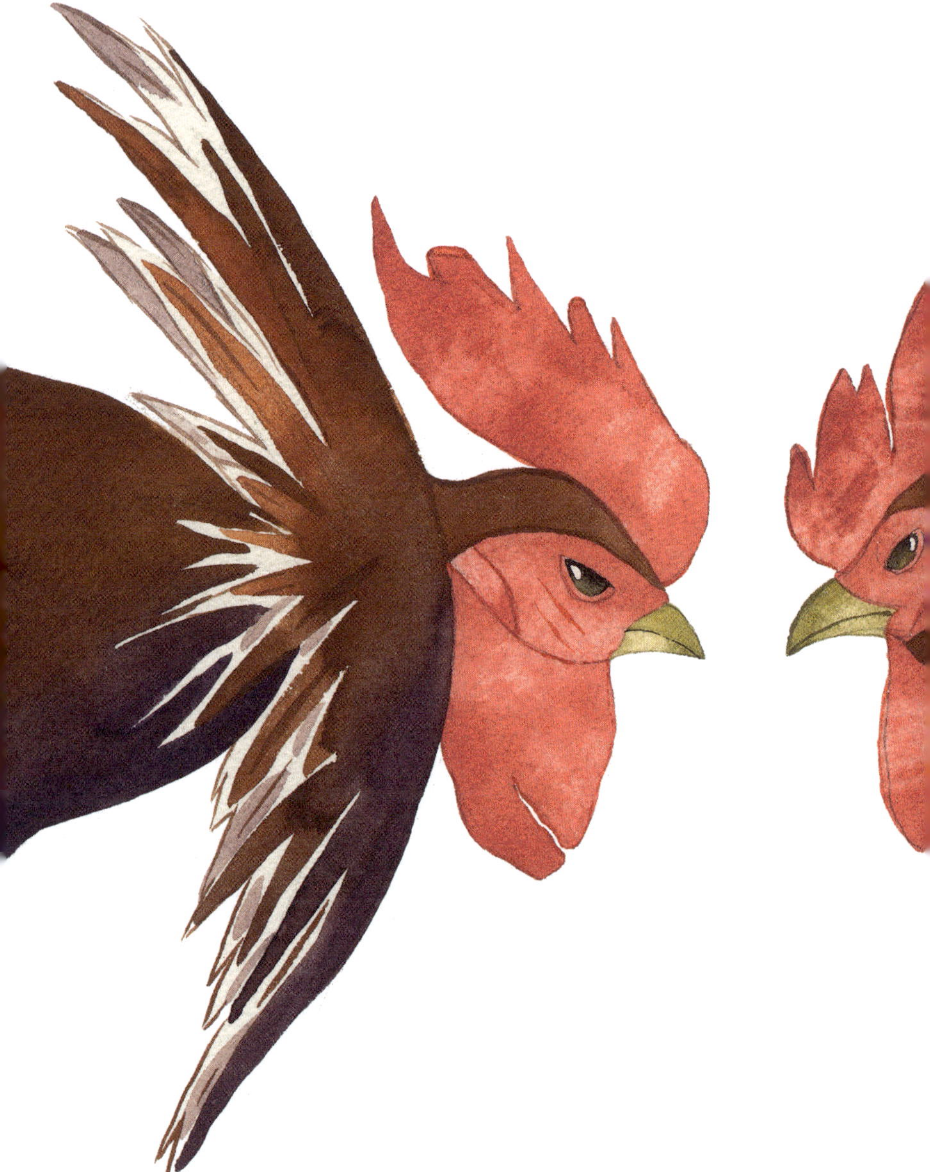

Raised hackles

Nowadays every agitated dog, cat, keyboard warrior or Saturday-night boozer has hackles that are very easily raised. This phrase goes back to the early 1800s, when barbaric cock fighting was a legal pastime. The specially-bred combative birds would have to be readied for battle, and once the feathers on the bird's neck (known as hackles) were raised, bloodshed would commence.

Rare as hen's teeth

Having wings, laying eggs and having a beak without teeth is what makes a bird a bird. So this old American phrase is describing something that is not only hard to find, it's probably impossible. Certain vinyl records, books, antiques, affordable housing in London: 'rarer than hen's teeth, mate.'

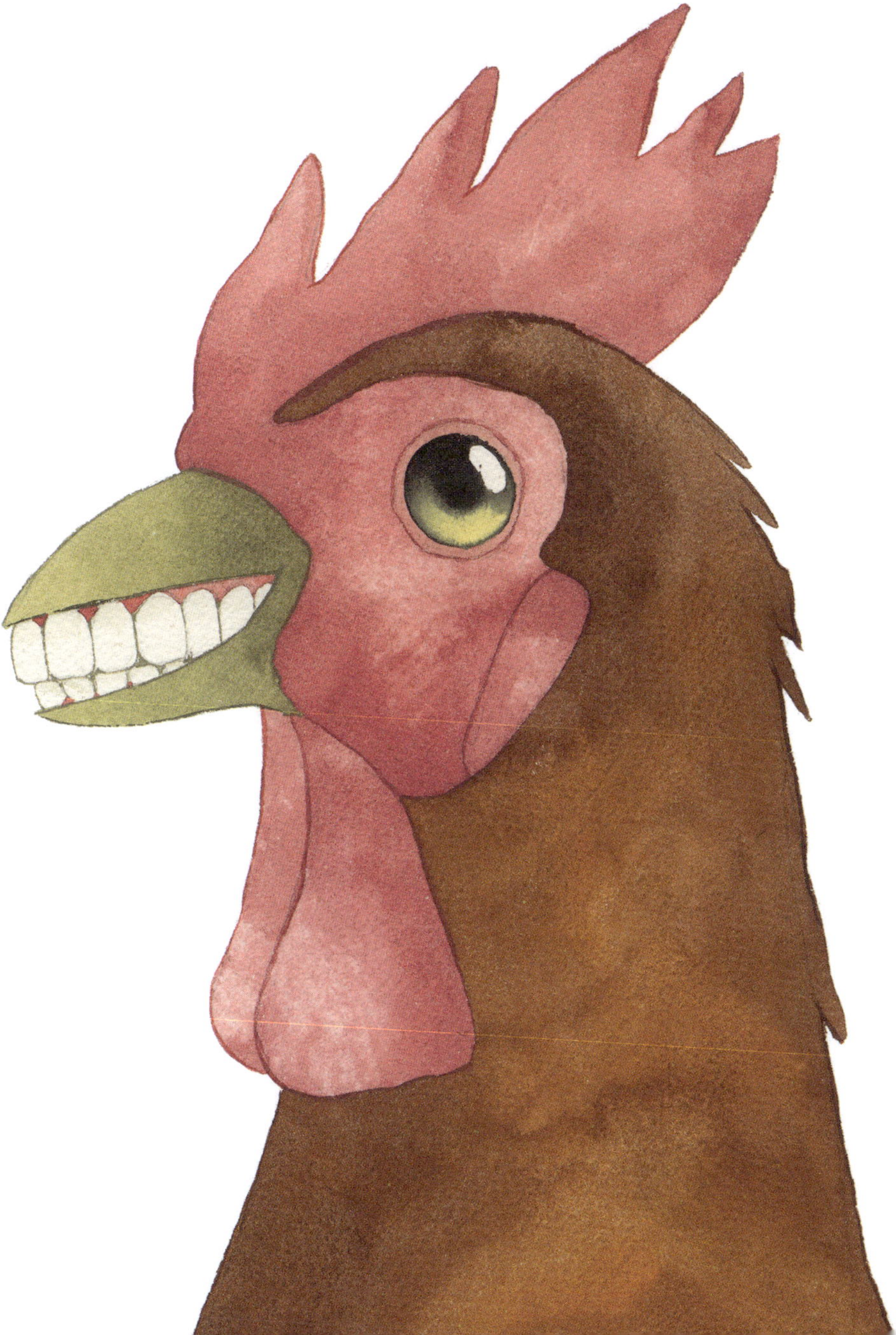

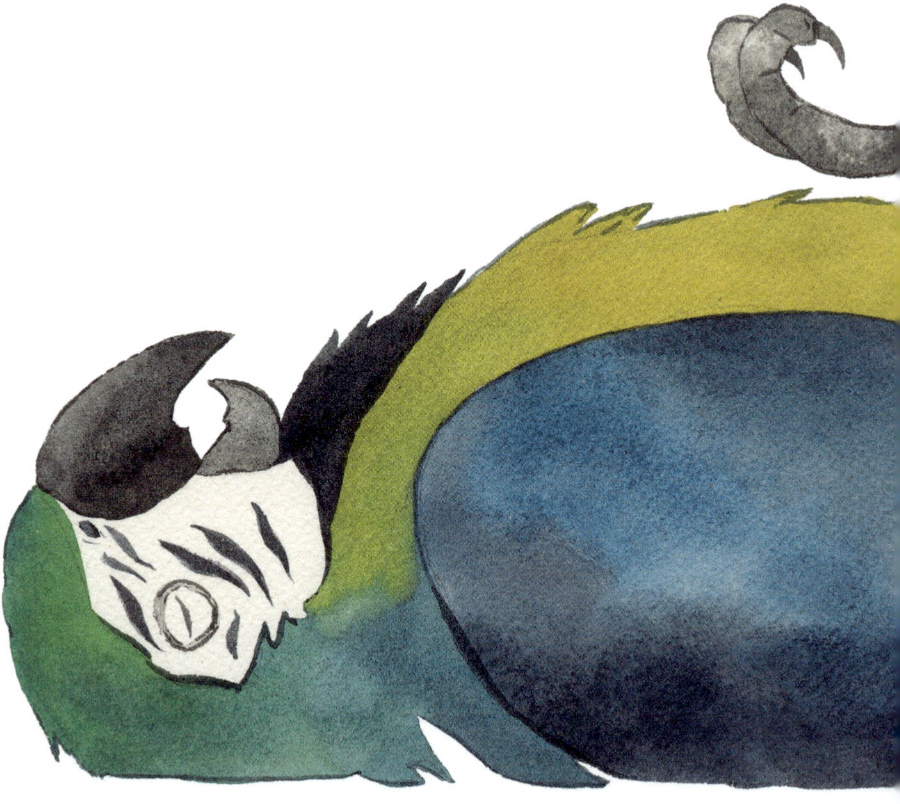

Sick as a parrot

Thought to have originated from a 1600s play, the phrase is also linked with the famous 'dead parrot' Monty Python's Flying Circus comedy sketch and is particularly commonly used in Australia. I guess they have a lot of them there! It's a great phrase as a poorly parrot is quite a depressing sight, sadly appearing almost like their vibrant colour is dripping off their beautiful wings.

Sitting duck

North American in origin, this idiom describes anything that's defenseless, vulnerable or an easy target. Like an unlocked bike outside a pub, the last sausage on your plate, or a duck sat or swimming rather than in flight, making it an easy shot for a hunter.

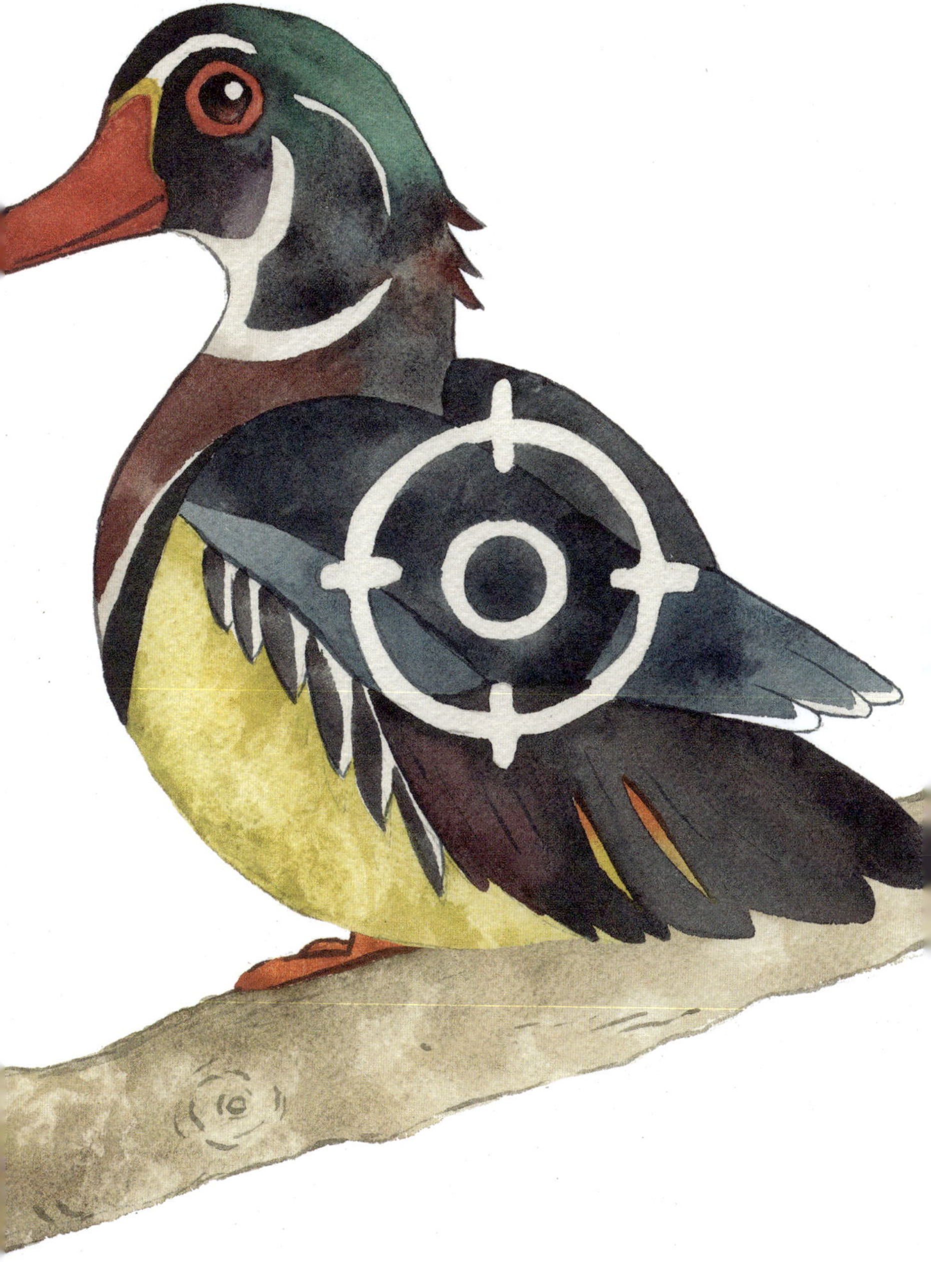

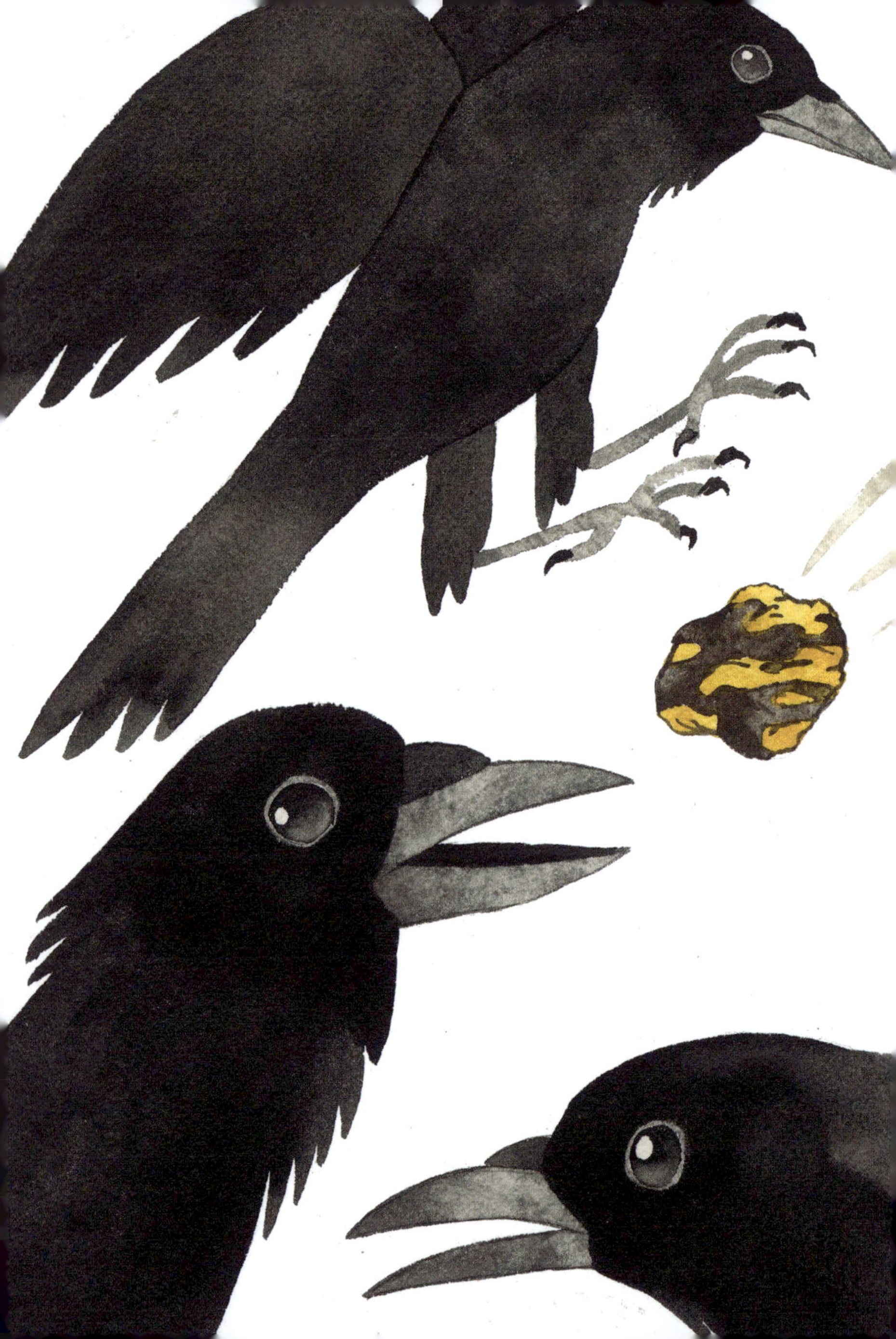

Stone the crows

...is a popular Australian expression of shock and amazement that originates from 1929, with the paperwork to prove it. A newspaper from Perth reports that boys had been employed to startle birds away from a newly planted crop. Being a stone-throwing human scarecrow was a tiresome pocket-money raising activity at the time, but to the boys' amazement one of them discovered, mid-throw, a big nugget of gold. Crikey!

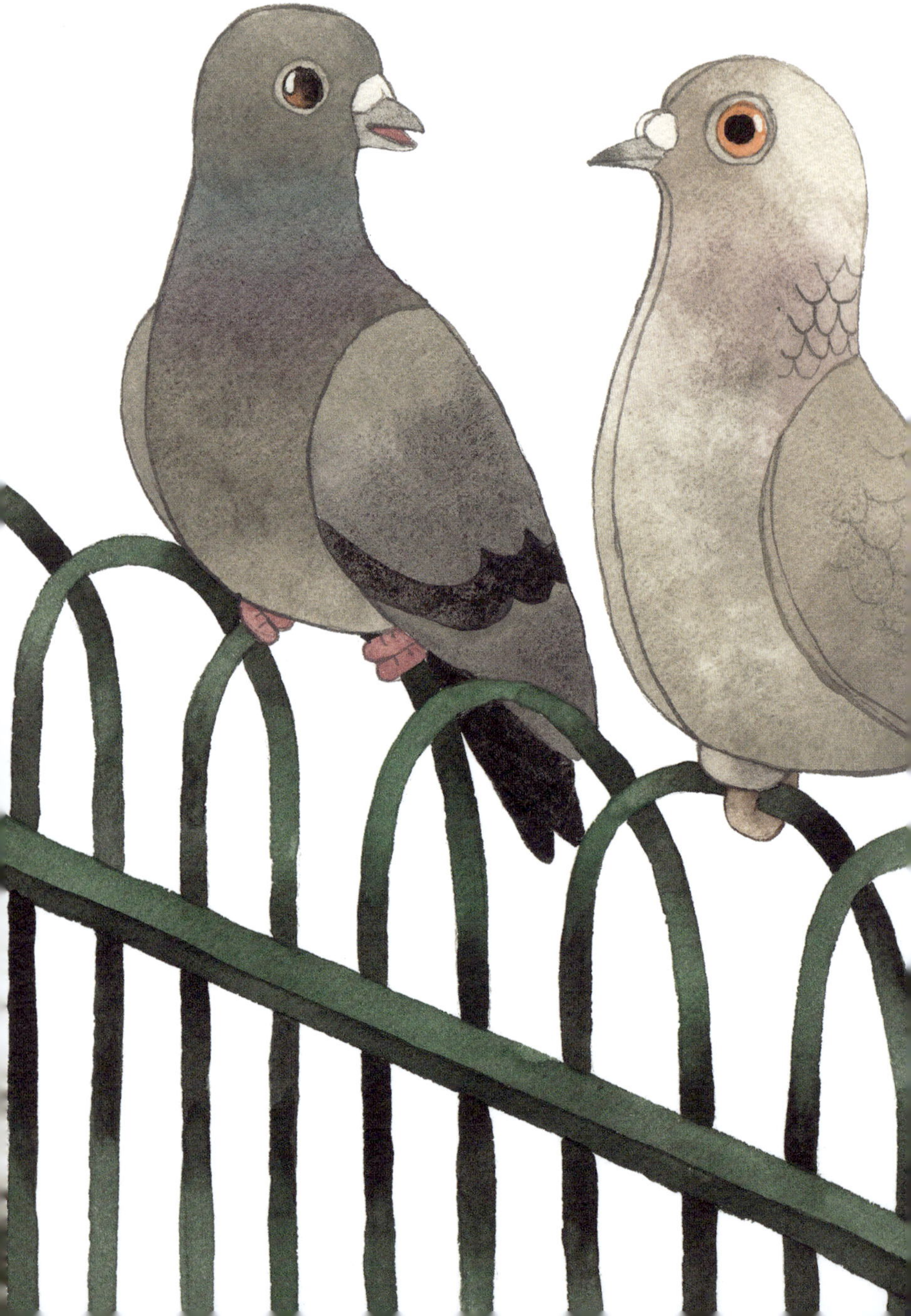

Stool pigeon

I've watched enough gangster movies to know that those fellas like to meet up and talk a lot, just like pigeons love to hang out and yak. Back in the 1800s, when pigeon was a mainstay on the menu, a live pigeon would be tied to a stool to attract a large flock to be easily netted. Over the years this evolved into wooden and then plastic fake birds. A similar tactic is used by police enforcers using known criminals as informants and spies. Those chatty gangsters are sitting ducks.

Thin as a rail

The rail family are a group of noisy but stealthy wetland birds. I always thought it was their long, skinny legs that the idiom refers to, but on inspection the bird's laterally-compressed body is incredibly thin width-wise, allowing it to pass quickly and unseen like a ninja through the tall marsh grasses.

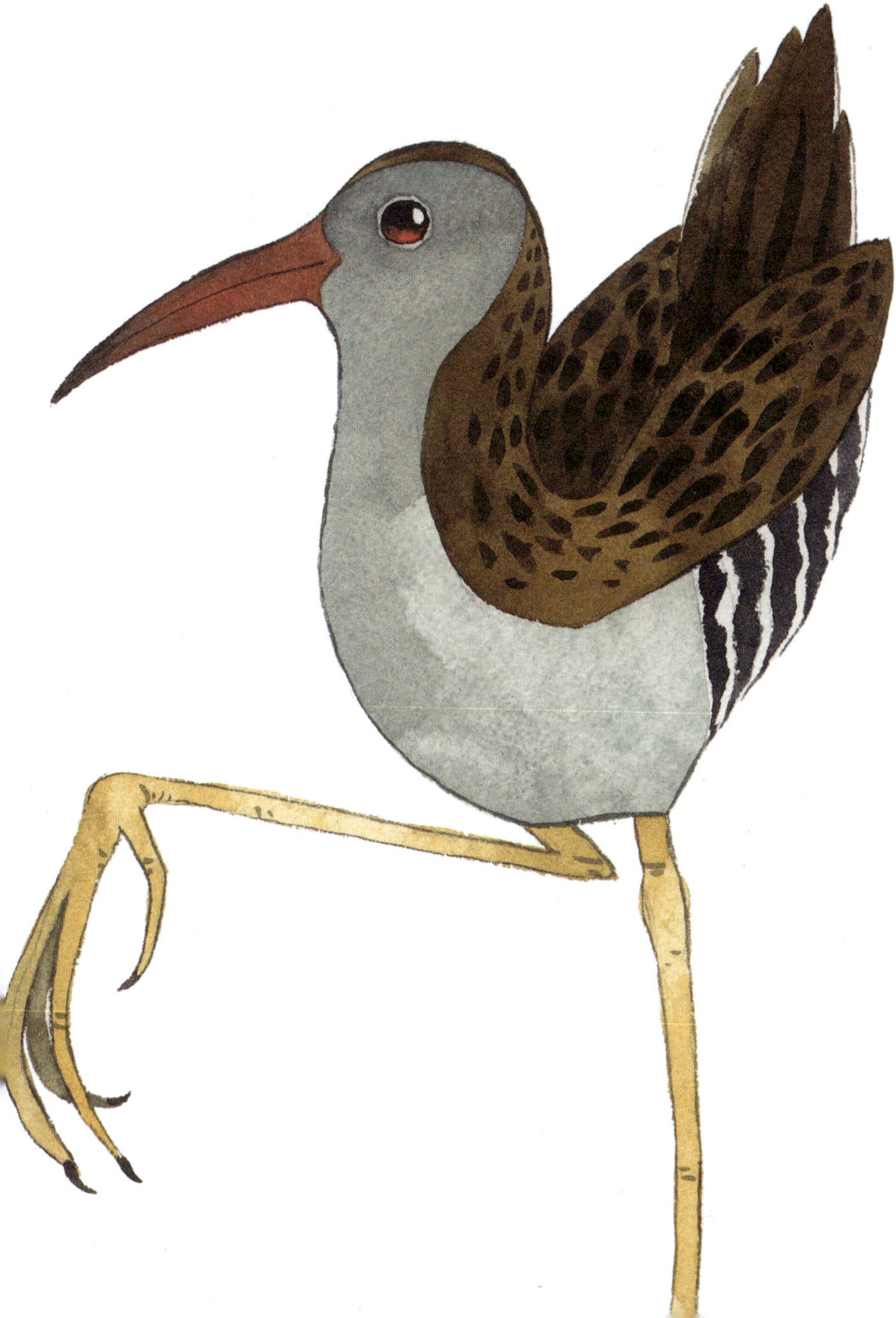

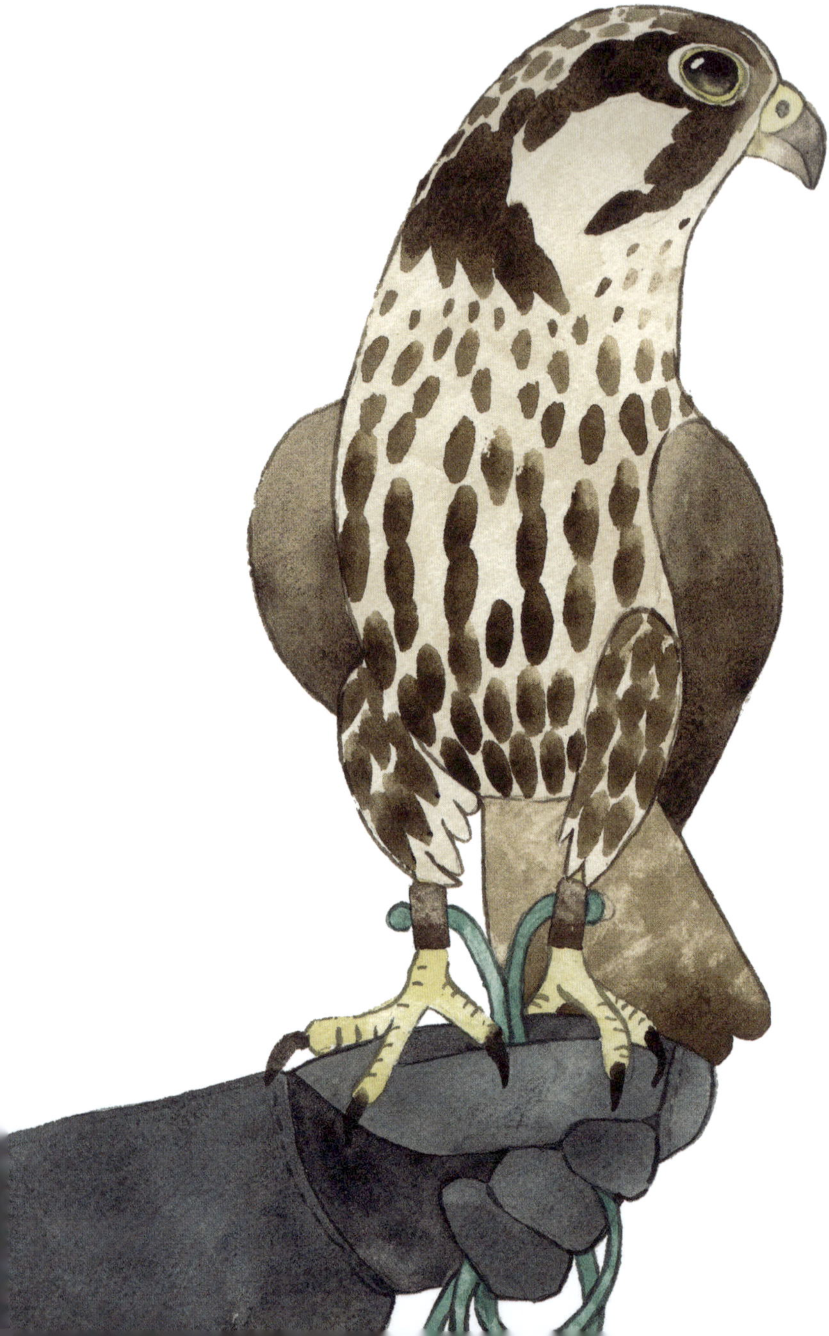

Under someone's thumb

Falcons and hawks may be hard to train, but once you have their tether under your thumb or wrapped around your finger, it is impossible for them to go anywhere. The same can be said about some of our relationships. It's funny to think that a phrase about manipulation and control, and one that feels so current, can be traced all the way back to medieval falconry.

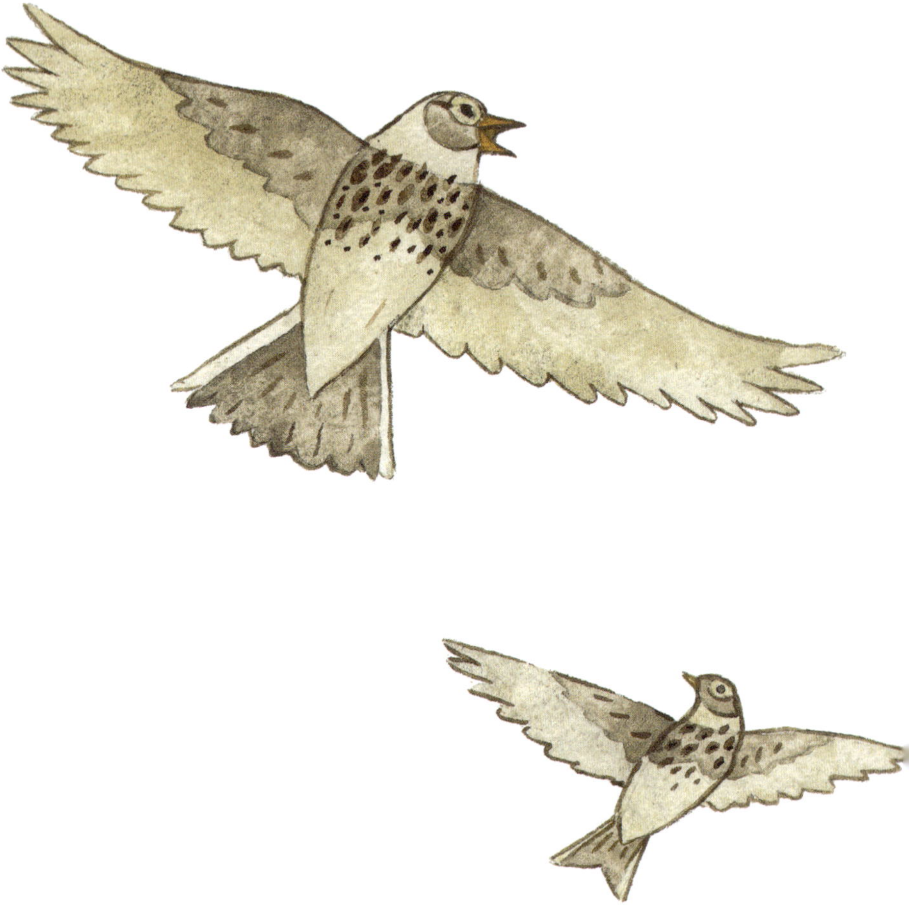

Up with the larks

An untraceable old English folk phrase that would have come from the fields and farms of the countryside, as that's where larks, in particular skylarks, can be found, from dawn, up in the air singing. Actually, not just singing, but belting out an acid techno tune mid-joyful aerial display. Their merry pleasure has inspired poems and music and many more sayings, such as 'larking about' and the maritime 'skylarking'.

The vultures are circling

Possibly one of the last things many a poor desert creature has seen before shuffling off this mortal coil is that of a boiling circle of vultures that have spotted their next meal. Being a bit ugly and displaying repulsive eating habits have given vultures a bad rep, but like other scavengers they are essential waste disposal and hygiene experts vitally important to our ecosystem.

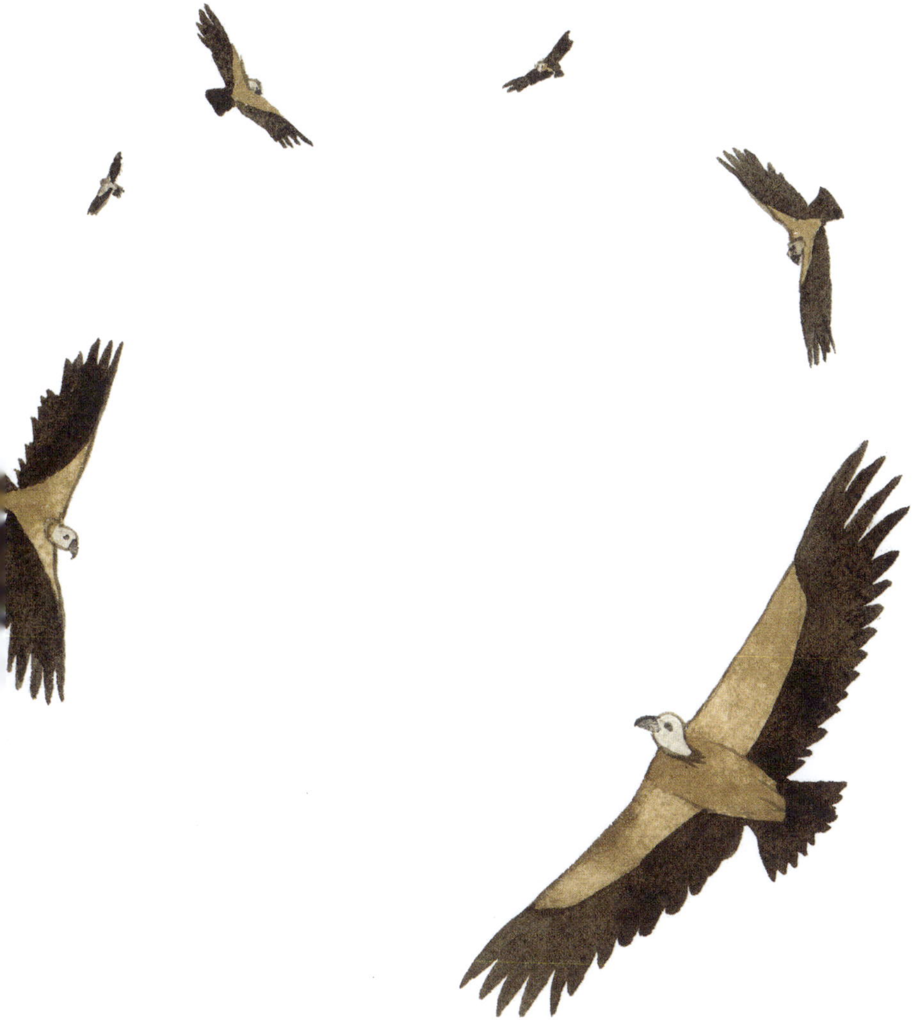

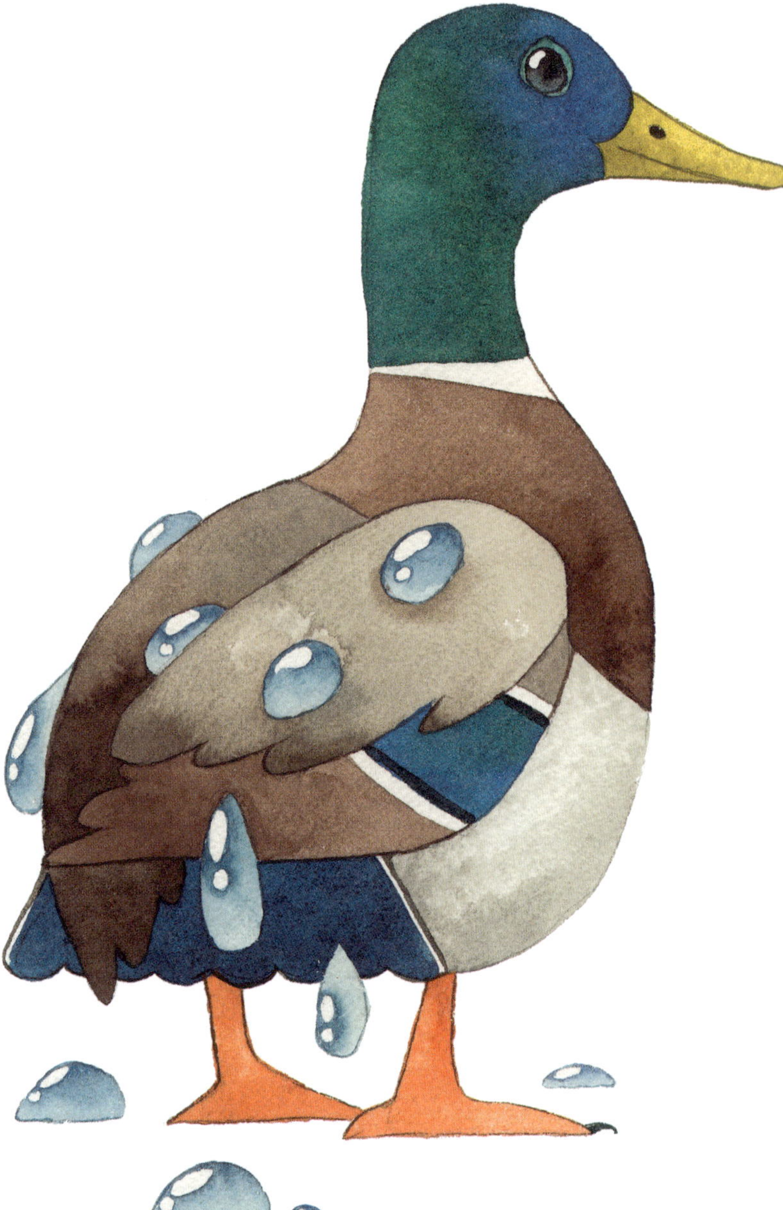

Water off a duck's back

To do something with such carefree abandon that it is practically nonchalant is pretty much how a duck stays dry. Their special oily feathers are like a Goretex parka, keeping the waterbird warm. Water just serenely slips off them without a second thought.

You can't hoot with the owls all night and soar with the eagles in the morning

A lovely North American folk phrase that beautifully points out that you can only burn a candle at both ends for so long, whether that be working too hard or partying too much – or both! Slow down. You can't be a night owl and expect to be eagle-eyed in the morning.

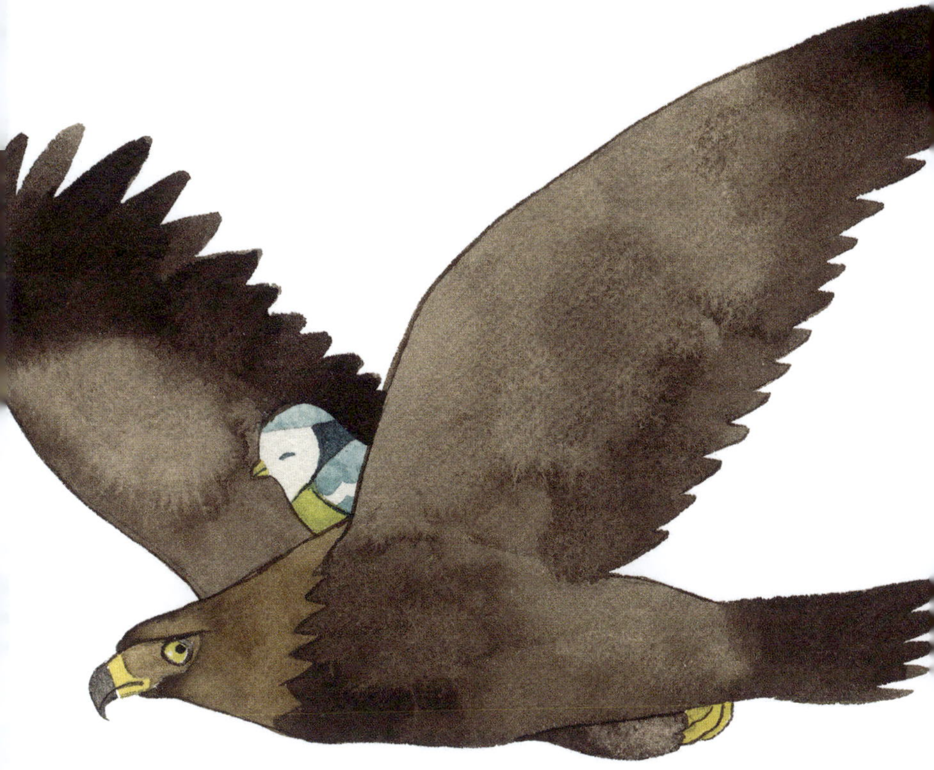

Acknowledgements

Thanks to Billy and Meg Meg, to Bill Cork and to Steph and her cousin for the gold.